DATE DUE

Demco, Inc. 38-293

Vassilios Bakoyannis

Paul: The Great Scandal
A Thought Provoking Message for the Contemporary World

Translated by Konstantine Papathanides

CONVIVIUMPRESS
SERIES SAPIENTIA

2 0 1 2

Paul: The Great Scandal

© Vassilios Bakoyannis

© Convivium Press 2012
All rights reserved
For the English Edition

http://www.conviviumpress.com
sales@conviviumpress.com
convivium@conviviumpress.com

7661 NW 68th St, Suite 108,
Miami, Florida 33166. USA.
Phone: +1 (305) 8890489
Fax: +1 (305) 8875463

Edited by Rafael Luciani
Translated by Konstantine Papathanides
Designed by Eduardo Chumaceiro d'E
Series: *Sapientia*

ISBN: 978-1-934996-34-8

Printed in Colombia
Impreso en Colombia
D´VINNI, S.A.

Convivium Press
Miami, 2012

No part of this book may be reproduced
or utilized in any form or by any means, electronic
or mechanical, including photocopying and
recording, or by any information storage or retrieval
system, without permission in writing from
the publisher.

«If your are not willing
to sacrifice yourself for your ideals,
then either your ideals are worthless
or you are worthless»

PLATO

Contents

Prologue PAGE 17

PART ONE

1
The Apostle's Youth PAGE 23

1. *The Apostle Paul's Family* PAGE 23
2. *His Education* PAGE 24
3. *His Studies in Jerusalem* PAGE 25

2
Jesus was a threat to Judaism PAGE 25

1. *Pentecost* PAGE 26
2. *Paul is Enraged* PAGE 27

3
Christian Persecution PAGE 27

1. *The Trial and Execution of Stephen* PAGE 28
2. *Persecutor and Murderer* PAGE 30

4
Paul's Unforeseen Conversion PAGE 31

1. *Something to Reflect Upon* PAGE 33

5
Why was Paul sent to Ananias? PAGE 34

6
Initial Reactions PAGE 36

1. *In Jerusalem* PAGE 37
2. *Paul is Summoned* PAGE 38

7
Where and How he Preached PAGE 39

1. *Urban Centers* PAGE 40
2. *Written Sermons* PAGE 40
3. *His Expenses* PAGE 41

8
«Bloody» Sermons PAGE 42

9
Paul was not God PAGE 43

10
The «Secret» PAGE 45

PART TWO

1
In Cyprus PAGE 49

1. *Paul Humiliates Elymas the Sorcerer* PAGE 50
2. *Mark Deserts the Apostles* PAGE 51

2
The Journey to Galatia PAGE 52

1. *Paul Contracts Malaria* PAGE 53

3
The Sermon in Galatia PAGE 53

4
Iconium PAGE 56

1. *Onesiphorus Greets the Apostles* PAGE 56
2. *The Uprising of the Idolaters* PAGE 57

5
The Apostles in Lystra PAGE 58

1. *Dramatic Events* PAGE 58
2. *Paul is Stoned* PAGE 59
3. *The End of Their Stay* PAGE 60

6
Disputes Over the Law PAGE 61

1. *The Apostolic Synod* PAGE 62

7
Paul's Disagreement with Peter and Barnabas PAGE 63

8
The Apostles and The Holy Spirit PAGE 66

PART THREE

1
The Beginning of His Second Journey PAGE 71

1. *In Troas* PAGE 72
2. *A Message From Macedonia* PAGE 72

2
In Philippi PAGE 73

1. *Paul is Beaten and Imprisoned* PAGE 74

3
The Apostles in Thessalonica and Berea PAGE 76

1. *The Apostles in Berea* PAGE 78

4
In Athens PAGE 78

1. *Paul's Discussions in the Market place* PAGE 79

5
Paul's Speech at the Areopagus PAGE 81

1. *Part One* PAGE 82
2. *Part Two* PAGE 83
3. *Part Three* PAGE 83

6
Conclusion PAGE 84

1. *The Athenians Had a Problem* PAGE 85

7
Paul in Corinth PAGE 87

1. *Paul Leaves Corinth* PAGE 89

PART FOUR

1
The «Overtaking» of Ephesus PAGE 93

1. *Ephesus* PAGE 93
2. *Ephesus is «Overtaken»* PAGE 94

2
The Public Uprising in Ephesus PAGE 95

1. *The Public Uprising* PAGE 96

3
The Epistles from Ephesus PAGE 98

1. *The Epistle to the Galatians* PAGE 98
   1.1. A TRUE APOSTLE PAGE 99
   1.2. CHRIST AND THE MOSAIC LAW PAGE 99
2. *The First Epistle to the Corinthians* PAGE 100
   2.1. THE «ELDERS» PAGE 100
   2.2. FACTIONS PAGE 101
   2.3. A TRUE APOSTLE PAGE 101
   2.4. CONCERNING SEXUAL IMMORALITY PAGE 102
   2.5. CONCERNING SPOUSES PAGE 103

4
News from Corinth PAGE 103

1. «I speak (…) foolishly…» PAGE 105

5
Raising Money in Corinth PAGE 106

1. An Attempt is Made on His Life PAGE 107

6
Paul in Troas and Miletus PAGE 107

1. Paul Bids Farewell to the Elders PAGE 108

7
The Journey to Jerusalem PAGE 109

8
Jerusalem is in Uproar PAGE 111

9
Paul is sent to Caesarea by Night PAGE 114

10
The «Warped» Governor PAGE 117

1. Felix meets Paul PAGE 117

11
Paul is Tried PAGE 118

12
Paul's Case PAGE 121

1. *Boarding the Ship* PAGE 123

13
The Journey to Rome PAGE 123

1. *In Malta* PAGE 126

14
In Rome PAGE 127

1. *A Warm Welcome for Paul* PAGE 127
2. *Under Arrest* PAGE 128
3. *An Unexpected Visit* PAGE 129
4. *Paul Grieves Over Barnabas* PAGE 130

15
The Sermon in Chains PAGE 130

1. *The Jews* PAGE 131

16
The Epistles Written while in Custody PAGE 132

1. *The Epistle to the Ephesians* PAGE 132
2. *The Epistle to Philemon* PAGE 133
3. *The Epistle to the Philippians* PAGE 134
   - 3.1. LIFE AND DEATH PAGE 134
   - 2.2. ADVICE PAGE 134
4. *The Epistle to the Colossians* PAGE 135
   - 4.1. SOLID FOUNDATIONS: SPIRITUAL STRUGGLE PAGE 135
   - 4.2. A CLEAN BODY PAGE 136
   - 4.3. A CLEAN SOUL PAGE 136

17
Paul is Acquitted: A New Beginning PAGE 136

1. *Paul Continues Preaching!* PAGE 137
2. *Paul in Spain* PAGE 138

18
Paul Bids Farewell to the Churches PAGE 138

1. *The Epistle to Titus* PAGE 139
2. *The First Epistle to Timothy* PAGE 139
3. *Nicopolis* PAGE 140

19
Paul's Last Moments PAGE 141

1. *Paul Arrives in Rome* PAGE 142
2. *Paul Asks for Timothy* PAGE 143
3. *Paul is Beheaded* PAGE 144

Conclusion PAGE 147

Prologue

One of the most incredible events to take place in the Church was the conversion of the Apostle Paul, the former Christian persecutor («terrorist») who became Christ's chief Apostle. His turnaround was so unforeseen that Ananias could not believe his ears when God told him to go and meet the Apostle Paul! (Acts 9:11-14).

What brought about this drastic change? Paul came face to face with the All-Mighty Lord!

Paul set off like a *«roaring lion»* (1 Peter 5:8), even though he had difficulty walking and was plagued by illness, to preach Jesus Christ who had risen from the dead to the far reaches of the world. He «crushed» idols and terrorized demons he came across along the way. Nothing could get in his way.

The former persecutor of Christ became a pillar of the Church. The majority of the New Testament books were written by Paul and his disciples. St. Luke was one of his disciples, as was St. Mark for a short period of time. Two of the four Gospels were written by Paul's disciples. Acts was also written by St. Luke. The New Testament is also comprised of fourteen of the Apostle Paul's epistles.

The Apostle's teachings are superior to great compositions such as the *Philokalia,* the *Gerontiko* and *The Ladder*, not to mention the teachings of modern day fathers (no matter how respected their teachings are). Even the lives of the great Saints of our Church do not compare to his life.

Even though we know much concerning the lives of modern day fathers, we know little about the life of the Apostle Paul[1]. This book looks at the life and teachings of the holy Apostle, the lamb that tamed the lion. He was truly a phenomenon. We hope you enjoy reading it.

---

1 Cf. JOSEPH HOLZNER, *Paul*, Athens 2001, 509, 21st Edition. The first Greek translation was done in 1950 by Archbishop Hieronymos I (+1988) of the Church of Greece. An English TRANSLATION is available by Scepter Publishers, 2002; Cf. ARCHIM. IOEL GIANNAKOPOULOS, Ἀρχιμ. Ἰωήλ Γιαννακοπούλου, Πράξεις Ἀποστόλων, ἔκδοσις δευτέρα, ἐκδόσεις Βασ, Ρηγοπούλου, Θεσσαλονίκη 1978.

Part One

1
The Apostle's Youth

«I am a Jew from Tarsus, in Cilicia, a citizen of no mean city» (Acts 21:39). Cilicia was a fertile plain on the coast of Asia Minor where wheat and fruit was grown. Tarsus was at the center of world trade and linked Eastern and Western civilizations at the time. Tarsus was well known for its highly acclaimed universities which could be easily compared to those of Alexandria and Athens. Wealthy families sought teachers from Tarsus for their children's education.

Alexander the Great hellenized the greater area, which meant that the Greek language and culture had a strong presence in Tarsus. There were also many Jewish immigrants who preserved their own culture. They were so strongly united that they made up a state within a state. They followed their religious obligations to the letter (circumcision, gathering at their synagogue, the learning of the Old Testament and above all, the Mosaic Law).

At the time, the Roman Empire had spread to almost the entire known world. In an attempt to Romanize the Hellenistic East, the Empire offered Roman citizenship to the people (Roman citizenship was considered a title). Roman citizens throughout the empire who were being tried had the right to appeal, which meant the trial was stopped and they were tried in Rome.

1.1. THE APOSTLE PAUL'S FAMILY

Although the Apostle's family was registered in Tarsus, they were also Roman citizens, which proved to be decisive for Paul (Acts 22:28-29).

Paul's mother died when he was young. He grew up with his father and sister who eventually married and moved to Jerusalem (Acts 23:16). His family spoke Greek at work and at home and so were bilingual (they spoke Hebrew and Greek).

Paul's father was a fabric merchant and a tentmaker. Certainly, Paul must have learned his father's trade when he was young (which helped him during his apostolic mission). His father was a member of the Pharisees, which meant that he passed on his beliefs to his son. The Mosaic Law was a way of life for Paul. He said he was «*of the tribe of Benjamin, a Hebrew of the Hebrews… a Pharisee*» (Philip. 3:5).

1.2. HIS EDUCATION

Primary education began at home at the age of five until the age of ten. Children were taught the significance of religious holidays (Passover, Pentecost, the feast of the Tabernacles), Mosaic Law (Deut. 5:6) and Psalms 113-118 which were chanted during holidays.

At the age of six, children went to school next to the synagogue. Children were picked up from their homes by their pedagogue (a servant who accompanied a child to school). He held their books in one hand and took them by the other hand, leading them to school through the busy city streets. For four consecutive years, children were taught the history of Israel (that Israel was God's chosen people). They were taught that the Messiah would come one day and that the entire world would be subject to Him. Even the Emperor of Rome would bow before Him and worship Him!

Secondary education began at the age of ten and ended at the age of fifteen. Students were taught numerous oral teachings concerning the law that were considered to be just as valid as the Ten Commandments. By this point in time, Paul had learned the Old Testament by heart (the Septuagint). Upon graduating from university, he knew the Old Testament by heart.

Post secondary education began at the age of fifteen. Students were taught the Talmud (a highly specific «set of rules»). Paul completed his studies, having learned the details of the Talmud.

1.3. HIS STUDIES IN JERUSALEM

Paul's father wanted his son to reach further heights so he sent him to Jerusalem for further studies. His teacher was Gamaliel, «*a teacher of the law held in respect by all the people*» (Acts 5:34). Paul was enchanted by his teacher's wisdom and ethics. Students would sit on the ground or on short stools in a semi-circle around their teacher. Paul would sit near his teacher's feet (Acts 22:3).

While he was a student in Jerusalem, Paul had close ties with the Synagogue of the Freedmen, which was made up of Judeans from Hellenist areas (Acts 6:9). Paul[1] would visit the synagogue on Saturdays and would listen to sermons and teachings which strengthened his faith even more. The members were certainly familiar with Paul's wealthy, merchant and Pharisee father.

Upon the completion of his studies, Paul returned to Tarsus. His zeal for his faith continued to grow. «*And I advanced in Judaism beyond many of my contemporaries in my own nation, being more exceedingly zealous for the traditions of my fathers*» (Gal. 1:14). Paul was a member of the Pharisees. «*They knew me from the first, if they were willing to testify, that according to the strictest sect of our religion I lived a Pharisee*» (Acts 26:5). Paul was becoming a zealot. He was considered an expert on Mosaic Law.

2
Jesus was a Threat to Judaism

When Paul was studying in Jerusalem, Christ had not begun his public mission. He was still unknown and living in Nazareth. Paul therefore did not meet or see Christ. When

---

1 There were approximately five hundred synagogues in Jerusalem at the time (which meant there was a synagogue on almost every street in the city!), all of which were filled to capacity with Moses' «followers». This was the environment in which the Apostle Paul was educated.

Christ began preaching and performing miracle after miracle, Paul was in Tarsus. Paul heard of what Jesus was doing but what concerned him above everything else was whether Jesus was an opponent of Judaism or not. When it was confirmed that Christ respected Judaism (He attended Jewish feasts, Passover, the Tabernacles, Pentecost), Paul felt reassured. Paul was also informed that Christ was crucified and that His disciples stole His Body so as to claim that He had risen from the dead (Matt. 28:11-15). Paul definitely must have felt reassured when he heard the news.

2.1. PENTECOST

The major feast of Pentecost happened to take place fifty days after Christ's Resurrection. Many Judeans from Pontus, Asia Minor, Cappadocia and Mesopotamia were in Jerusalem for the feast (Acts 2:9). Paul's relatives Andronicus and Junia were also in Jerusalem. The Holy Spirit descended on the Apostles and they preached Christ to the masses. Moses was no longer their leader! Christ was their new leader! The people instantly believed and three thousand people were baptized (Acts 2:41), among whom were Paul's relatives and fellow countrymen, Andronicus and Junia (Rom. 16:7).

Christ's new religion had gained so much momentum the number of faithful was growing day by day. «*The number of the disciples multiplied greatly in Jerusalem*» (Acts 6:7). The number of the faithful multiplied to 24,000! A large number of priests also followed the faith (Acts 6:7)! The well-known Cypriot Levite Joses, who was a friend of Paul's, was one of them (Acts 4:36). His name was changed to Barnabas (which means son of encouragement). The faithful were united so strongly, it was as if they all shared one heart and soul. Their love for each other was so great, they shared all of their possessions (Acts 4:32).

2.2. PAUL IS ENRAGED

Paul was eventually informed of the events that were taking place in Jerusalem. He could no longer tolerate hearing that the law was being annulled by a deceased convict (Jesus)! A specific verse from Scripture constantly came to his head: «*For anyone hung on a tree is under God's curse*» (Deut. 21:23). It was impossible for a cursed man to be the Messiah, thought Paul. Jesus posed a threat and had to be dealt with!

Paul's obsession with the word «*cursed*» did not allow him to see the numerous prophecies that foretold of the Crucifixion and Resurrection of the Messiah. He decided to put an end to Jesus' «presence» and hastily made his way to Jerusalem. He knew that he would definitely have the support of the government because Roman law protected Judaism. This meant that Christ's followers were guilty because they were a threat to Judaism. Paul, therefore, had the right to persecute and kill them!

3
Christian Persecution

Christianity was divided into three groups at the time. The first was comprised of people who were born and raised in Jerusalem. They were Jews who believed that Christ came to save their people and only their people. The second was made up of Jewish people who were born outside of Palestine (hence they had Greek names like Stephen, Philip, Andrew etc.) but moved to Jerusalem. They were indifferent to the Mosaic Law. The third group was made of up idolaters who had become Christians (Gentiles). Being former idolaters, they had nothing to do with Mosaic Law. The increasing numbers of Gentile Christians was a threat to Judaism. Paul was not concerned about Jewish Christians because they followed the Mosaic Law[2]. It was the other groups he was concerned about because they were his mortal enemies!

3.1. THE TRIAL AND EXECUTION OF STEPHEN

The archdeacon Stephen who was «*full of faith and the Holy Spirit*» (Acts 6:5), went to the synagogues and preached Jesus Christ, who had risen from the dead, to his fellow Hellenist Jews. One day, while he was preaching in the synagogue of the Freedmen, Paul arrived. His fellow countrymen (who knew of his educational background) were anxious to see how he would react upon hearing Stephen's preaching. The synagogue was full to capacity.

Upon hearing Stephen's teachings, the crowd (including Paul) became outraged. Instead of experiencing feelings of peace and tranquility, they stopped him and a heated discussion began. Each side put forth its arguments. Paul certainly must have spoken out against him and made references to Holy Scripture. Stephen, on the other hand, definitely must have referred to scripture, pointing out that the Messiah had to suffer first and then be glorified. There is no doubt that the people must have continued to argue against Stephen and that Stephen continued to provide answers to their arguments, thus silencing them (including Paul). They could not bear to hear such words. They falsely accused Stephen of turning against the Law of God (which was considered the most serious accusation of all against Jewish people).

The people's rage against Stephen reached its peak. They seized him and took him to be tried. Paul was among the crowd. False witnesses took to the stand and accused Stephen of blasphemy against the faith, the temple and the law. «*This*

---

2 When Paul was on trial in Caesarea, later on in his life, he thought of a way for Christianity to be considered a fulfillment of Judaism so as not to make it seem a threat to Judaism. Paul stated that Judaism preached the coming of the Messiah, as foretold by the prophets. He then stated that Christianity preached the arrival of the Messiah, thus making Christianity a fulfillment of Judaism. Paul, therefore, was not an adversary of Judaism by preaching Jesus Christ (Acts 24:13-15).

man does not cease to speak blasphemous words against this holy place and the law; for we have heard him say that this Jesus of Nazareth will destroy this place and change the customs which Moses delivered to us» (Acts 6:13-14).

Stephen quietly listened to the accusations made against him. Suddenly, his face glowed so radiantly, he looked as if he were an angel (Acts 6:15). This was the best evidence that the accusations made against him were false (his teachings were true). One would have expected his accusers to stop and consider the spectacle; however, they were so obsessed and blinded that they could not see the light shining before their very eyes!

The high priest Caiaphas, who was accustomed to such unjust trials, was somewhat concerned about the sight (the fact that his face was glowing) and asked Stephen: *«Are these things so?»* (Acts 7:1) Stephen replied: *«Brethren and fathers, listen…»* Stephen began his defense. He explained that their forefathers had done wrong in the past by being at enmity with the prophets and killing them. He explained that this was the case with Jesus of Nazareth. He called on them to stop doing what they had done in the past but they were fixed in their ways. Stephen went on the attack and said to them: *«You stiff-necked and uncircumcised in the heart and ears! You always resist the Holy Spirit; as your fathers did, so do you. Which of the prophets did your fathers not persecute? And they killed those who foretold the coming of the Just One, of whom you now have become the betrayers and murderers»* (Acts 7:2-52).

Paul, Caiaphas and everyone present became outraged. According to law, anyone making a mortal man God was to be stoned (Lev. 13:9-10) outside of the city (Lev. 24:4). In other words, anyone preaching that Jesus Christ was God was guilty and deserving of death. Stephen said to them: *«Look! I see the heavens opened and the Son of Man standing at the right hand of God»* (Acts 7:56). He did not say «I think» but «*I see*». Those present covered their ears so as not to hear the «blasphemous» words spoken by Stephen. They seized him and took him outside of the city to stone him (Acts 7:57-58).

The people made Paul the «supervisor» of Stephen's execution. He was to oversee the execution and he gave the people instructions on what to do. According to the law, the first people to throw stones at him were the people who directly heard his words (witnesses). Paul was one of them and he threw the first stone at Stephen. He then stepped aside and overlooked.

The other witnesses placed their clothes at Paul's feet (perhaps in order to be able to move more freely) and continued throwing stones at Stephen's body and head. The stones tore his body and head open. There was blood everywhere. Paul had taken revenge and was pleased at the sight. Stephen prayed while he was being stoned: «*Lord Jesus, receive my spirit*» (Acts 7:59). Moments before his death, Stephen found the strength to pray for those who were killing him. He cried out: «*Lord, do not charge them with this sin*» (Acts 7:60). He then died.

3.2. PERSECUTOR AND MURDERER

Stephen's martyrdom was the beginning of a long period of pain and martyrdom for the new Church of Christ. Supporters of Judaism were set on eradicating Christianity so as to preserve and save their faith from Jesus, who was a threat to them. With Paul as their leader, they declared war against Christianity. The barbaric persecution of Christianity thus began (Acts 8:1-3) with Paul at the helm.

The Sanhedrin devised a secret plan to wipe out Christianity. They had people bear false witness against Christians, thus turning the general public against them. New songs which reinforced religious and national sentiments were composed. When the situation was difficult, Paul would appear to reinforce the fight and to strengthen the people's faith.

A special court was also established and Paul was appointed head. He was the leader of the fight against Christianity. He put together a well organized group of dedicated people who worked night and day. Armed policemen would enter the homes of Christians and place them in reformatories which were beneath the numerous synagogues that existed. They were beaten, whipped (the law foresaw 39 lashes for offenders) among other things, in order to make them deny Christ. Those who refused to comply were taken to court, convicted and executed (with Paul's approval!).

Even though large numbers of people were tortured and killed, Paul was not satisfied. He wanted more blood and more deaths (Acts 9:1). He wanted to go to Damascus and bring back Christians who had escaped from him and fled. He took epistles written by the chief priests to show to the synagogues in Damascus so that he could take any Christians he found back to Jerusalem. Paul got on his horse and set off for Damascus with the epistles in hand. He would arrive in approximately one week (little did he know that Christ had set up an «ambush» and was waiting for him along the way…).

Many Christians fled to Phoenicia, Cyprus, Antioch (Syria) and Damascus (which was full of Hellenist Jews) as a result of the harsh persecution of Christianity (Acts 11:19). Ananias (one of Christ's seventy disciples) was among those who had fled to Damascus.

4
Paul's Unforseen Conversion

«*People on earth make plans and God looks at them from Heaven and laughs!*» God was about to to change Paul's plans. Instead of taking Christians captive, God was about to take him captive and make him His servant.

Paul was approaching Damascus. He was riding through the lush plain of Damascus which was full of fruit trees. As he approached the city, his thirst for blood grew greater. He had been travelling for a week and expected to be compensated for his lengthy journey by bringing back as many Christians as he could.

The sky was completely clear. Suddenly there was lightning and thunder. A bright Light (Christ's glory) shone on Paul. The light was brighter than the sun! Paul got off his horse and fell to the ground. He then heard a voice (Christ) speak to him: «*Saul, Saul*[3], *why are you persecuting Me? It is hard for you to kick against the goads*» (Acts 9:4-5). Note that Christ did not speak to Paul in an abrupt manner. He spoke to him kindly and gently. He even called his name twice! (as He did when he called Moses, see Exod. 3:4).

«*Who are You, Lord*», asked Paul (Acts 9:5) «*I am Jesus, whom you are persecuting*» (Acts 9:5). The Lord then told him to rise (Acts 9:6). «*But rise and stand on your feet; for I have appeared to you for this purpose, to make you a minister and a witness of the things which you have seen and of the things which I will yet reveal to you*» (Acts 26:16). Paul got on his feet, but he could not see.

Paul was then converted! Everything happened so suddenly. There was no dialogue and he did not resist whatsoever. Paul's turnaround was certainly unexpected.

How did this unforeseen event take place? How could this be possible?

Paul believed that he was persecuting a cursed man. When he realized that he had been persecuting God he was in shock. He could no longer continue persecuting Christians after his meeting with the Lord of Glory. He did an about face within fractions of a second. He was enchanted by Christ's presence. The Lord did not hinder Paul's ability to decide for himself when He appeared to him. Paul was able to think and judge for himself. He could have said «no» to Christ but he chose to be obedient. «*Therefore King Agrippa, I was not*

---

[3] Saul was Paul's name in Hebrew. Paul was the name he used in honour of the Roman proconsul Sergius Paulus in Cyprus, whom he met during his visit there.

disobedient to the heavenly vision…» declared Paul later on (Acts 26:19).

4.1. SOMETHING TO REFLECT UPON

Let us assume that before entering Damascus, Paul had had conversation with the greatest and wisest people of his time. Would they have been able to change his mind? Stephen, who was full of wisdom and grace and shone like an angel could not do so, so it is safe to assume that no person could have changed Paul's mind. Have you ever heard of anyone as fanatic as Paul change his mind upon hearing a few simple words? Christ's personal intervention (which was discreet so as not to breach Paul's personal will, thus allowing him to decide) brought about the unexpected change in Paul. This is a perfect example of how discreet the Lord is in His actions and words.

Did Paul actually see and hear Christ or was he hallucinating? Was it all merely a dream? We need to recall that it was noon and Paul was on horseback. There was no way it could have been a dream. Let us assume he was dreaming. Would such a fanatic have changed his mind so quickly after seeing a dream? There was no way a Pharisee like Paul who was so highly educated would have believed in a dream. Furthermore, if Christ were dead, would He have performed such a miracle? Would He have appeared before Paul and converted him into His Apostle? Have any mortal individuals done anything similar? Has anyone (who was dead) ever appeared before someone who opposed them and transformed them into an avid follower of his?

Paul's conversion is distinct. Jesus Christ was triumphant over death through death and lives! He is not simply alive but He is the All-Ruling Lord who is omnipresent and overlooks everyone and everything. He can change anything and everything with the utterance of a few words!

5
Why was Paul sent to Ananias?

«*Arise and go into the city, and you will be told what you must do*» (Acts 9:6), said the Lord to Paul. He was led to Ananias, surely an odd instruction!

Why did God not tell him to go directly to Ananias? Instead, he told him to go into the city and wait for further instructions.

Christ always acts with wisdom and discretion. He always takes our psychological state into account. Ananias was on Paul's «most wanted» list. Would Paul have been able to bear hearing that he was being told to go to Ananias? In addition, Christ told him that he would be told what to do. Why did Christ not tell him what to do directly? Could Christ not have told him what to do?

Christ did all that He had to do for Paul! He called on him and gave him instructions, which is something no one else could have done (not even the presbyter Ananias nor an entire Ecumenical Synod for that matter). However, God sent Paul to Ananias for further instructions in order to show us that we should not await instruction from above (from Heaven) but we must humble ourselves and ask Christ's «representatives» (His clergy, priests, spiritual fathers) for instructions, according to scripture: «*Ask your father, and he will inform you; ask your elders and they will tell you*» (Deut. 32:7).

Even though Paul was face to face with the Lord Himself, he did not ask Him for further information but humbled himself and followed the instructions of a presbyter who he was planning on executing! This is exactly why the Apostle Paul reached the spiritual heights he did!

What happened next? The guards who accompanied him on his journey took him by the hand (he could not see) and continued on their way to Damascus. They made their way through the lush woods and through the Gate of Saul. They continued along the straight avenue which was approximately one kilometer in length and thirty meters wide and had impressive Corinthian pillars on both sides, and entered the city.

They were given accommodation by a fellow countryman named Jude. Still in shock, Paul locked himself in his room, refusing to eat or drink anything. Three days had passed and he was still blind (Acts 9:8-9). God sustained his blindness in order to open the eyes of his soul and make him think deeply and he did so…! However, being human, he anxiously awaited the day after.

The Lord judged (after three days) that it was time for Paul to meet Ananias and regain his sight, thanks to Ananias! God informed both of them concerning their meeting. The Lord showed Paul a vision in which Ananias touched him and he received his sight. The Lord appeared before Ananias and told him what to do: «*Ananias. Arise and go to the street called Straight and inquire at the house of Judas for one called Saul of Tarsus, for behold he is praying. And in a vision he has seen a man named Ananias coming to him and putting his hand on him, so that he might receive his sight*» (Acts 9:10-11).

Ananias could not believe his ears, regardless of the fact that God was speaking to him! This was so because Paul was infamous and greatly feared for his harsh persecution of Christians. «*Lord, I have heard from many about this man, how much harm he has done to Your saints in Jerusalem. And here he has the authority from the chief priests to bind all who call on Your name*» (Acts 9:13-16). Even so, Ananias showed obedience to the Lord and met Paul. Paul did nothing but listen to his words. «*Brother Saul, the Lord Jesus, who appeared to you on the road as you came, has sent me that you may receive your sight and be filled with the Holy Spirit*». Ananias placed his hand on Paul's head and a scale like substance fell of his eyes. Paul received his sight (Acts 9:17-18).

Paul was baptized in the name of Christ. He finally had something to eat and stood on his feet. He remained in Damascus for a few days, together with the Christians of the city

(Acts 9:17-19). He embraced them. Initially, the Christians of Damascus could not believe what had happened!

Paul retreated to the Arabian wilderness in preparation for his apostolic mission (Gal. 1:17) where he fasted, prayed and studied Scripture. He remained there for approximately three years (from 33-36 AD). His body resembled that of a skeleton due to his strict fasting. Everyone must certainly have wondered what had happened to him for he had vanished and there was no trace of him.

6
Initial Reactions

Paul returned to Damascus after spending three years in isolation in order to preach Jesus Christ, whom he had persecuted so severely. Damascus was the home of many Jews. This was a major problem that Paul would have to face.

The Christians of the city did not pose a threat to him for they would eventually believe him. However, the Judeans of Damascus were a serious threat to Paul because many of his former collaborators were in Damascus. When the Lord appeared to Paul, He informed him of what he would face in the future: «*I will deliver you from the Jewish people, as well as from the Gentiles…*» (Acts 26:17).

Paul appeared in the synagogues and preached that Jesus was the Son of God (Acts 26:20). All present were shocked! «*Is this not he who destroyed those who called on this name in Jerusalem, and has come here for that purpose, so that he might bring them bound to the chief priests?*» (Acts 9:21). They shouted and threatened him but he was not alarmed one bit. He continued teaching with the same zeal, «*proving that this Jesus is the Christ*» (Acts 9:22).

Seeing his courage and strength, the Jews decided to kill him! They were aware of the fact that he would be returning to Jerusalem and so they watched the gates of the city night and day. Paul was informed of the plot, as were the Christians of Damascus who did everything they could to help him. At night, they let him down the wall of the city in a basket. Paul ran into the fields, disappearing into the night![4]

6.1. IN JERUSALEM

When Paul arrived in Jerusalem, the first thing he did was meet up with the Christians of the city (Acts 9:26). Imagine how surprised they must have been. He explained what had happened to him and he spoke to them from the heart concerning Jesus, the Son of God. They were reluctant to believe him: «*And when Saul had come to Jerusalem… they were all afraid of him, and did not believe that he was a disciple*» (Acts 9:26). They thought he was trying to fool them.

His friend from childhood Barnabas who was kind and full of the Holy Spirit (Acts 11:24), approached him, talked to him and came to the conclusion that Paul was being sincere. He then presented him to the Apostles Peter and James (Acts 9:27). Peter, who was bold and impulsive, was ecstatic when he heard of the miracle. He embraced and kissed Paul. Paul remained with them for fifteen days (Gal. 1:9).

One can only imagine what they discussed. Peter, being an eyewitness, told him everything about Christ. Paul told him about his conversion. Paul must have been eager to see where Christ was born, crucified, buried and resurrected.

Upon seeing Peter together with Paul and hearing Barnabas verify that Paul had changed, the Christians of Jerusalem were now certain that Paul was a brother of theirs.

Paul's thoughts now centered on his friends and his former colleagues (who stoned the protomartyr Stephen). He wanted to speak to them concerning Christ and he wanted

---

[4] The Lord could have helped Paul escape with the help of an angel, as would seem fit for one of His worthy servants. He did not because God wants us to think and act on our own. God intervenes when we are unable to protect ourselves. From now on, Paul would be in constant danger. He would have been inundated with pride if the Lord sent an angel to help him every time he was in danger.

to lead them to repentance. He preached to them and held discussions with them in public. They were enraged and wanted to kill him (Acts 9:29). They also threatened all the Christians of the city.

Paul could see that his preaching was having no effect and was grieved as a result. He wanted to offer Christ something after having persecuted Him so harshly.

One day, when Paul was praying in the temple, he heard the Lord say: *«Make haste and get out of Jerusalem quickly, for they will not receive your testimony concerning Me»* (Acts 22:18). Paul replied: *«Lord, they know that in every synagogue I imprisoned and beat those who believe on You. And when the blood of Your martyr Stephen was shed, I also was standing by consenting to his death…»*. The Lord said: *«Depart, for I will send you far from here to the Gentiles»* (Acts 22: 19-21).

Paul secretly left Jerusalem. He bid farewell to Peter, James, Barnabas and all of his brothers in Christ (with mixed feelings). He went to Caesarea, where he remained for a while (Gal. 1:22) and made his way to his homeland, Tarsus (Acts 9:31). He remained in isolation for five years (37-42 AD). He felt like a lion in a cage. He hoped that things would change and that he would be able to preach Jesus Christ, whom he had seen with his own eyes. The city of Antioch (Syria), which had a population of a half a million people, was waiting for the Apostle!

6.2. PAUL IS SUMMONED

The Church in Jerusalem sent Barnabas to Antioch in order to examine the problems of the local Church there. When Barnabas, who labored for the Glory of Christ (not for his own personal glory) saw the problems in Antioch, it dawned on him that his friend Paul was the only individual who would be able to deal with a city so large. Barnabas went to Tarsus to find Paul (Acts 11:25). *«And when he had found him, he brought him to Antioch. So it was that for a whole year they assembled with the church and taught a great many people»* (Acts 9:26).

And so, Paul began his God-given mission at the age of forty. He was the Apostle of the Gentiles. His odyssey began in Antioch. He preached Jesus Christ for 23 years (from 45 AD to 68 AD), travelling the seas and crossing different lands!

His education (he was an expert on Scripture and a teacher of the Law) and the fact that he was a former persecutor of Christ meant he was the most unique teacher for the task. He made masses of Gentiles see the light. When the Lord first appeared to Paul, He told him to «*open their eyes, in order to turn them from darkness to light, and from the power of Satan to God…*» (Acts 26:18).

7
Where and How He Preached

By the seventh century BC, the Judeans had begun to spread to different parts of the world. They took their faith with them wherever they went. They were known as Hellenist Jews. During the Apostle Paul's lifetime, Judeans could be found throughout the Roman Empire (Cyprus, Asia Minor, Greece, North Africa, Palestine, Syria, Galatia etc.). When Paul arrived in a city, he first met with his fellow countrymen and then had them assemble in their synagogues to preach to them. He began by referring to the Old Testament teachings and prophecies and eventually preached Christ, who suffered, was buried and rose from the dead.

When he preached to idolaters, he first referred to the creation as a natural revelation of God. Then he referred to the conscience which leads us to become acquainted with God, the creator of the world, and then he referred to God who became man, was crucified and defeated death through death by resurrecting Himself.

Being a Hellenist Jew, Paul spoke Greek and Hebrew. When he preached, he did so in Greek because it was the common language at the time (as a result of the conquests of Alexander the Great). Greek was spoken throughout the Roman Empire, even in Rome itself. The Apostle Paul's epistles were written in the Greek language (even his epistle to the Romans).

7.1. URBAN CENTERS

Since it was impossible for the Apostle to preach in every town and village, he preached in large busy cities (Athens, Corinth, Thessalonica, Rome, etc.). He preached in towns and villages only in his homeland (Asia Minor, ex. Pamphylia, Iconium, Antioch, Troas, Miletus). Why did he not preach in Alexandria (the second largest city of the Roman Empire)? It is likely that he had heard that Mark was preaching there. Paul also made a rule of not building on the foundations set by others: «*And so I have made it my aim to preach the gospel, not where Christ was named, lest I should build on another man's foundation...*» (Rom. 15:21).

Paul's mission was not limited to preaching. When he finished preaching in a city, he remained there and baptized all who believed in Christ. If the entire city believed, he baptized the entire city. From what can be interpreted, he did not baptize people himself but had his colleagues perform the sacrament (1 Cor. 1:14) while he continued preaching. «*For Christ did not send me to baptize, but to preach the gospel...*» (1 Cor. 1:17). Those who were baptized needed a presbyter. He carried out the Divine Liturgy, ordained ministers, preached, guided them and answered their questions. In this way, he established local Churches in places where the Church was not present.

7.2. WRITTEN SERMONS

When the Apostle could not visit the Churches he had established, he sent epistles to them. Some of his epistles were lost. «*I wrote to you in my epistle not to keep company with sexually immoral people*» (1Cor. 5:9). This is evidence that his first epistle to the Corinthians (as we know it) is actually not his first. He sent the Corinthians a previous epistle before 1 Corinthians[5]. He sent four epistles to the Corinthians, two of which were lost. His epistle to the Laodiceans was also lost (Col. 4:16). Fourteen of his epistles remain.

His epistles were read in church during the Divine Liturgy, which all Christians attended. His epistles brought about discussion among Christians and his opponents alike. Even his opponents found his epistles impressive: «*For his letters are weighty and powerful, but his bodily presence is weak, and his speech contemptible*» (2 Cor. 2:10). Paul's reply to this comment was: «*What we are in word by letters… such we will also be in deed…*» (2 Cor. 10:11).

7.3. HIS EXPENSES

Paul was in need of money in order to buy food, to pay rent, to pay for his journeys, etc. Being an Apostle and Shepherd of the people, he could have asked to be supported by Christians of the local Church where he was staying (as was the case with the other Apostles, see 1 Cor. 9:8-12). He did not want anything to interfere with his preaching, which is why he did not ask local Churches for financial support (1 Cor 9:12). He said: «*And I will not be burdensome to you; for I do not seek yours, but you*» (2 Cor. 12:14). He worked to pay for his expenses (he was the only Apostle to do so).

Wherever Paul went, he was hard at work. He made tents out of the most difficult material to work with (material made of camel or goat hairs). This enabled him to pay rent, buy food for him and his colleagues, pay fares when they travelled and pay the inns they stayed at. He often worked from morning to night (he did not work part-time). «*For you re-*

---

5 The Apostle Paul dictated most of his epistles (he did not write them himself) (1 Cor. 1:1). His hands were full of calluses from making tents (1Thess. 2:9) so he had difficulty writing. When in Rome he was imprisoned and in chains, therefore, he could not write (2Tim. 2:9) the four epistles which he sent from there (Ephesians, Philippians, Philemon, Colossians).

member, brethren, our labor and toil; for laboring night and day, that we might not be a burden to any of you, we preached to you the gospel of God» (2 Thess. 2:9).

8
«Bloody» Sermons

The Apostle Paul worked harder than any other of Christ's Apostles! No one preached in as many cities as he did (he walked over 5,000 km). He was persecuted and imprisoned for the sake of preaching Christ more than anyone else. Paul preached Christ just as passionately (if not more so) as he persecuted Him.

The Apostle walked from destination to destination. Sometimes he walked for a month on his weary feet to reach his next destination. On most occasions, he was hungry and thirsty. He wore few clothes, even when travelling in the winter. On some occasions he was practically naked! (2 Cor. 11:27). *«For I think that God has displayed us, the apostles, last, as men condemned to death; for we have been made a spectacle to the world. To the present hour we both hunger and thirst, and we are poorly clothed, and beaten, and homeless. We have been made as the filth of the world...»* (1 Cor. 4:9-13).

He walked difficult routes. He treaded on rocky paths, walked along cliff-sides, passed through mountains in the snow and crossed rivers (2 Cor. 11:26). He often came across robbers and on many occasions, his life was threatened! *«I have been in the deep; in perils of waters, in perils of robbers... in perils in the wilderness, in perils in the sea...»* (2 Cor. 11:26).

He stayed at inns while traveling, where he slept on stiff beds made of camel or goat skin on wooden planks. Blankets and utensils were not provided at the inns (it was the travelers obligation to have his own) so he had to carry his belongings with him (blankets, plates, knives, forks etc.) from place to place. The quality of sleep at these inns was not the least bit satisfactory. There were insects present, not to mention the calls and grunts of animals that were near. He stayed at such inns on numerous occasions. As a result, he was sleepless many a time (2 Cor. 11:27).

Paul was not exactly welcomed in every place he preached. He was threatened by his own countrymen and by Gentiles alike. «*From Jews five times I received forty stripes minus one. Three times I was beaten with rods; once I was stoned; three times I was shipwrecked; a night and a day I have been in the deep*» (2 Cor. 11:24-26). In the end, he was decapitated. What more could he have done for Christ?

9
Paul was not God

Although Paul was a vessel of the Holy Spirit and could heal the sick by touching them with his garments (Acts 19:11), he was not God. Regardless of how holy and great he was, he remained a mortal human with weaknesses and imperfections. (We must not confuse imperfect people with God.)

As long as man is alive, he is burdened, whether he likes it or not, by bodily passions (sleep, labor, hunger etc.) and passions of the soul (cowardice, grief, anxiety etc.). Even Christ's human nature possessed the same passions. Paul stood firm with respect to bodily weakness (2 Cor. 11:27), for he was often sleepless, hungry, cold and practically naked. He stood his ground well. However, it seems that he could not withstand the passions of the soul. It is important to recall that even Christ was unable to pray when He contemplated His Passion which awaited Him. He stopped praying and went to His disciples for comfort (Matt. 26:39-45)! If we take into account the fact that Paul was very emotional, it is easy to understand why this «giant» was overcome by passions of the soul. «*What do you mean by weeping and breaking my heart?*» (Acts 21:13).

Paul may have been able to withstand the threat against him in Damascus and Jerusalem and he may have been able to withstand the persecution and imprisonment he faced after but there were times when God permitted the «giant» (the Apostle Paul) to break. There were times when Paul resembled a completely different person.

On certain occasions, Paul was encouraged by local Christians (people who were spiritually inferior to him, see Acts 28:15). There were times when he felt extreme loneliness. When he was alone in Athens, he told his brethren to send those who were accompanying him (who were in Macedonia) to Athens. After Paul had seen them for a while, he sent them back to Macedonia to shepherd their flocks. «*We thought it good to be left in Athens alone*» (1 Thess. 3:2-3).

«*But woe to him that is alone when he falls, and there is not a second to lift him up*» (Eccl. 4:10). Judas was alone after betraying Christ. He was full of self-loathing and committed suicide as a result. The Apostle faced a difficult situation when he was alone in Athens. He could not stand hearing the Athenians mock our holy faith, so much so that when he arrived in Corinth after leaving Athens he was «*in weakness, in fear, and in much trembling*» (1 Cor. 2:3). He had not overcome his grief when he set foot in Corinth! Paul, who had overcome so many hardships in Iconium, Lystra, Philippi, Thessalonica and Berea (persecution, beatings and being stoned) could not overcome the Athenians' reaction to his words!

His experience in Troas was just as surprising. Paul left Ephesus and headed to Troas, which was far away. Paul was anxious to see his disciple Titus but when Paul arrived in Troas, he was saddened to hear that Titus was not there. «*I had no rest in my spirit, because I did not find Titus my brother*» (2 Cor. 2:13). How exactly did Paul feel? Was he anxious or depressed? We do not know exactly. What we do know is that Titus' absence affected him so much he could not overcome it. When he went to preach (preaching was his life) he could not do so. He did not have the strength to preach to the people. He bid farewell to the people and left! He may not have had the strength to pray so as to overcome his feelings. He may have prayed (we are not certain) but even if he did so, he could not mange to overcome his feelings![6]

The most surprising aspect of this great man is that even though he was weak in body (he was ill) and soul (he was afraid, lonely etc.), he managed to travel to the far reaches of the world, preaching Jesus Christ to the world and bestowing the entire world to Christ's hands.

10
The «Secret»

«*A thorn in the flesh was given to me, a messenger of Satan to buffet me, lest I be exalted above measure*» (2 Cor. 12:7), said Paul. However, he did not specify what this «thorn» was. There are three interpretations of this verse.

The fist interpretation states that it refers to the temptation of lust. Is it possible that such a man faced such a temptation? Of course it is. The desire for lust always lurks within us. A wise modern day father, Epiphanios Theodoroupoulos (+1989), used to say that this temptation ceases only when we die.

There are people who experience this temptation but refuse to succumb to it. Temptation is different from the desire to sin. The first is considered natural and therefore, is not considered a sin (even with respect to holy people). Paul's temptation remained just that, a temptation. He had no desire to sin. Being experienced in spiritual combat, he was able to control it and God rewarded him for his efforts and struggles. Our view is that he did not face such temptations

---

[6] Imagine how spiritually inferior people are affected (taking into account how the Apostle Paul was affected) and how much support they require. «*Strengthen your brethren*» (Luke 22:32), said Christ to Peter.

because of the fact that he had burdened his body to the limit (2 Cor. 11:27).

The second interpretation refers to an individual who despised Paul so much, he burdened him during his apostolic mission. Some believe that this person was his wife! This could be true if he were a permanent resident of one city. Paul journeyed throughout the world for 23 years. This person could not have possibly followed him from place to place on his difficult journeys (from Cyprus to Galatia, Greece, Rome etc.). Let us assume that this person did follow him from place to place. Would his brethren have allowed for such a thing to happen? Would they not have supported their teacher?

The third interpretation refers to an illness. Paul was plagued by malaria, which meant he had a high fever, fatigue and extremely painful headaches. Why then did he make reference to «*a messenger of Satan*»? He himself preached that illnesses brought on the forgiveness of sins (1 Cor. 5:1, 32).

The reason behind this was that idolaters believed that the gods sent malaria to unclean individuals who dared to approach holy places. When idolaters came across someone having malaria, they spat on him because they believed it rid the person of his demon. Paul wanted to win idolaters over in the name of Christ; therefore he was not clear about the illness he had contracted.

Part Two

1
In Cyprus

It was spring of 45 AD. Paul had completed one year of his mission in Antioch (Syria) (Acts 11:25-30). Something was telling him that there were many nations sitting in darkness who were in need of seeing the Light of Christ. His friend Barnabas, who was with him in Antioch, had the same sentiments. The chief members of the local Church also shared the same feelings. Someone had to be sent to preach to the Gentiles.

Who would be chosen to carry out this mission and where would they go? Barnabas must have wanted to go to Cyprus. Would he leave his friend Paul behind? There were different views on the matter and no progress was being made. They fasted and prayed for God to reveal His will to them. The Divine Liturgy had just been completed and the chief members of the local Church gathered together to discuss the matter. Barnabas, Symeon called Niger, Lucius the Cyrene, Manaen (who had grown up with Herod Antipas) and Paul were present. Just as the five men were about to come to a decision, the Holy Spirit spoke to them, saying: «*Now separate to Me Barnabas and Saul for the work to which I have called them*» (Acts 13:2). (The Holy Spirit intervened, demonstrating that It was responsible for the decision). The dispute had now been settled. The members accepted the decision without any doubts.

The local Church fasted for the chosen Apostles once again (as it had fasted before the intervention of the Holy Spirit).

The Holy Spirit thus «deprived» Antioch of Paul and Barnabas. The local Church in Antioch was at a loss. However, the Church is not guided by people (if this were the case, it would have sunk a long time ago).

Paul and Barnabas took John Mark (the author of the Gospel according to Mark), Barnabas' nephew, with them.

They headed towards the port of Seleucia together with the clergy and the laity. Everyone bid farewell to Paul, Barnabas and Mark, venerating them, and returned to Antioch with mixed feelings. The three Apostles were on their way to Cyprus (Acts 13:4).

They reached Salamis, which was Barnabas' hometown. The city possessed the largest port in Cyprus. Salamis was on the eastern side of the island. This is where they began preaching (Acts 13:5).

1.1. PAUL HUMILIATES ELYMAS THE SORCERER

Darkness is the adversary of light. When light appears, darkness disappears. When light is absent, darkness rules. This was the case in Paphos, where the sorcerer Elymas ruled. When the Apostle Paul (light) set foot in Paphos, the darkness (Elymas) vanished.

Paphos, the capital of Cyprus (on the other side of the island), which was under the rule of the proconsul Sergius Paulus, was being rid of the sorcerer Elymas, who performed numerous miracles with the power of the devil. He enchanted the people and was considered a god by everyone, including the proconsul, who was an intelligent man (Acts 13:7).

Paul, Barnabas and Mark made their way across Cyprus (a distance of approximately 150 km). They arrived in Paphos after an exhausting five day journey. Their preaching was truly impressive. It was the first time the people had heard such words. The words of Elymas did not compare to those of the Apostles. The proconsul heard about what had taken place. He summoned Paul and Elymas to the palace for a «confrontation». Paul's face was full of hope and tranquility (the light of Jesus Christ). The proconsul was enchanted as result. Elymas did whatever he could to convince the proconsul not to give up his faith, for if he believed in Paul's words, the news would spread across the entire island.

Paul went on the counter attack. He said to him: «*O full of deceit and all fraud, you son of the devil, you enemy of all right-*

eousness, will you not cease perverting the straight ways of the Lord?» (Acts 13:10). A dark mist then fell on Elymas and he lost his sight. *«And now, indeed, the hand of the Lord is upon you, and you shall be blind, not seeing the sun for a time»* (Acts 13:11). Elymas looked for someone to take him home. The sorcerer who performed impressive miracles and signs was now helpless. The power of God had eradicated his (satanic) power.

Sergius Paulus, seeing the power of the True God preached by Paul, believed in Christ[1].

1.2. MARK DESERTS THE APOSTLES

Mark, Barnabas' nephew, was distressed by what he saw. It was the first time he witnessed such a bold man (Paul). Perhaps it was his belief that Christ came to save the Judeans only (in other words, he may not have agreed with their preaching to the Gentiles).

The three got into a boat and left Paphos for Perga in Asia Minor. As they approached the coast, they could see the Taurus Mountains getting larger and larger. Mark must have thought that Paul was set on crossing the mountain range. He came to the decision to leave the Apostles as soon as they set foot on land. He asked for his uncle's blessing. Surely the Apostles attempted to convince him to stay. They must have said to him: «The Taurus Mountains, are nothing in comparison to Christ's Passion. The harder we work for Christ, the more blessed we will be». Mark could not be convinced. Neither Barnabas nor the great Apostle Paul could change his mind. Mark left to the Apostle's dismay, for they had lost a colleague.

---

[1] Paul «honored» the proconsul for his belief by changing his name Saul (Hebrew) to Paul (Roman).

2
The Journey to Galatia

Galatia was a large area where different Greek speaking tribes lived (Celetes, Fryges, Pisidians, Lycaones). The Galatian king Amyntas united the tribes, thus creating a Galatian nation, which was subject to Rome. Antioch (Pisidia), which was beyond the Taurus Mountains, was the Apostles' next stop.

Antioch in Pisidia was nothing like Antioch in Syria. Antioch in Pisidia was at an altitude of 1200 meters (Antioch in Syria was at an altitude of 80 meters). It was a difficult place to find basic necessities for survival. It was a dangerous six day journey on foot from the port of Perga. Travelers had to pass through Pamphylia, which had many residents who had malaria. Travelers had to traverse the Taurus Mountains. The Apostles had to walk along cliff sides, cross rivers without bridges (which meant they had to get wet, along with all of their belongings). There was also extreme weather to deal with. There were blizzards and warm days. Travelers had to make certain they were near inns at nightfall, otherwise they risked freezing to death and being eaten by wild beasts.

Paul was informed concerning Pamphylia and the dangerous route that led to the inhospitable city of Antioch. Instead of avoiding going there, the Apostle went as quickly as he could. He was like a raging bull on Taurus Mountain. We must keep in mind that Paul had difficulty walking (he was slow).

He walked along cliff sides, reached the peaks of mountains, walked through blizzards, crossed rivers by walking or swimming across, faced robbers and had to sleep in abominable inns that smelled of animal dung. Even so, he was eager and ready to preach Jesus Christ. When he first arrived in the city, he sought his fellow countrymen and introduced himself and Barnabas. They in turn offered them accommodation. They must have expected to hear something important from them, especially since they had gone through so much to reach their city. News of their arrival spread to the surrounding towns. Paul and Barnabas were the center of attention.

2.1. PAUL CONTRACTS MALARIA

While he was passing through Pamphylia, he contracted malaria. He felt the first symptoms just as he was about to begin preaching. He could not walk nor could he stand. The «lion» was confined to bed (Gal. 4:13). He was concerned for he knew that idolaters were superstitious when it came to individuals who had malaria. How could he preach to them if they knew he had malaria?

The city residents were so overwhelmed by Paul that there was no way they would consider him to be cursed by the gods. When they saw how sick and exhausted he was, they wanted to help him as much as they could. Paul stated that they wanted to help him so much, they would have plucked out their own eyes and given them to him! (Gal. 4:14). They thought of him as an angel of God. Some even considered him to be Jesus Christ! (Gal. 4:15).

3
The Sermon in Galatia

It was Saturday and the Judeans of Antioch had gathered in their synagogue for their weekly prayer, reading from Scripture and discussion concerning Scripture. The rabbis, the ruler of the synagogue and the members of the council stood up front. The men stood behind them and the women stood behind the men, being separated by a wooden structure. Paul and Barnabas, together with proselytes who had gathered to hear the Apostles, stood in a designated area for strangers.

The reader took to the stand and read the first chapter of Deuteronomy and verses from Isaiah. The synagogue ruler sent someone to the Apostles who said: «*Men and brethren, if you have any word of exhortation for the people, say on»* (Acts 13:15). Everyone turned around and looked at the Apostles, wondering what these strangers had to say. What could they add to the teachings of the rabbis and teachers of the law?

Paul took the stand and motioned for quiet. He began by reminding them of how God had benefited the people of Israel: *«Men of Israel, and you who fear God, listen. The God of Israel chose our fathers, and exalted the people when they dwelt as strangers in the land of Egypt, and with an uplifted arm He brought them out of it. Now for a time of about forty years he put up with their ways in the wilderness... He raised up for them David as king... From this man's seed, according to the promise, God raised up for Israel a Savior —Jesus—»* (Acts 13:16-26).

«Men and brethren, sons of the family of Abraham, and those among you who fear God, to you the word of this salvation has been sent. For those who dwell in Jerusalem, and their rulers, because they did not know Him, nor even the voices of the Prophets which are read every Sabbath, have fulfilled them in condemning Him. And though they found no cause for death in Him, they asked Pilate that He should be put to death. Now when they fulfilled all that was written concerning Him, they took Him down from the tree and laid Him in a tomb. But God raised Him from the dead.

And we declare to you glad tidings-that promise which was made to the fathers, God has fulfilled this for us their children, in that He has raised up Jesus. As it is also written in the second Psalm: You are My Son, Today I have begotten You (Psalm 2:7). *You will not allow Your Holy One to see corruption* (Psalm 16:10). *For David... fell asleep, was buried with his fathers, and saw corruption; but He whom God raised up saw no corruption»* (Acts 13:26-37).

Paul's sermon then reached a critical point. He made references to Mosaic Law. He declared that salvation came only with Christ. He certainly drew their attention now. *«Therefore, let it be known to you, brethren, that through this Man is preached to you the forgiveness of sins; and by Him everyone who believes is justified from all things from which you could not be justified by the law of Moses. Beware therefore, lest what has been spoken in the prophets come upon you: Behold, you despisers, Marvel and perish! For I work a work in your days, A work which you will by no means believe, Though one were to declare it to you»* (Acts 13:37-41).

The Judeans boasted (until then) that they were the chosen people of God. Their fellow countryman, Paul was saying things that were not permitted to be said! He included the Gentiles in his teachings. Furthermore, he mainly spoke concerning Christ and made few references to Mosaic Law. Only Christ brought about salvation. On the other hand, the proselytes were enthusiastic when they heard him preach, for salvation was theirs also.

Paul and Barnabas left the synagogue so as to avoid any confrontations. The proselytes surrounded them and asked them to return on the following Saturday. The Apostles answered «yes» and the proselytes accompanied them to their place of accommodation together with some good-willed Judeans. The Apostles explained the words they heard in the synagogue and advised them to remain steady in the grace God had given them. The proselytes passed on news of Paul's teachings to friends and acquaintances. The people anxiously waited for Saturday to come (Acts 13:42-43).

Saturday finally arrived. The Apostles made their way to the synagogue where almost the entire city had gathered. Fanatic Jews could not bear to hear their words. They were enraged and as a result of Paul's teaching. *«It was necessary that the word of God be spoken to you first; but since you reject it, and judge yourselves unworthy of everlasting life, behold, we turn to the Gentiles. For so the Lord has commanded us»* (Acts 13:46-47).

«Now when the Gentiles heard this, they were glad and glorified the word of the Lord. And as many as had been appointed to eternal life believed» (Acts 13:48). The Gentiles spread the word to friends and relatives in the region. *«And the word of the Lord was being spread throughout all the region»* (Acts 13:50).

The fanatic Judeans were enraged. They had to do something to stop what was happening. They approached the prominent women of the city and they in turn convinced their husbands to expel the Apostles from the city (Acts 13:50-51). Upon leaving the city, the Apostles shook the dust off their feet, as the Lord had commanded them (Mat. 10:14).

4
Iconium

Iconium was at a distance of approximately 120 km from Antioch (a four- to five-day walk). The city stood at an altitude of 1030 meters on the banks of a lake. Iconium was inhabited by Galatians, Jews, Roman employees and veterans. The route leading to the city was not exactly welcoming.

The Apostles were faced with two choices. The first was the easier route to the west, which led to Ephesus. The second was to the east which led to Iconium. They decided to take the most difficult route of the two and made their way across the dry mountain plain that led to Iconium. It was a difficult journey.

The plain was full of dust during the dry summer months and the hot sun made it difficult on the feet. Finding water was another story. In the winter, the snow made walking impossible. In spring, the plain resembled a lake (water melted from the mountain tops and collected in the plain) and there was no way to get around the water, which was also deep. It is likely that the Apostles crossed the plain during spring (and therefore had an extremely dangerous journey).

4.1. ONESIPHORUS GREETS THE APOSTLES

Although God permits his servants to face difficult temptations, He sends relief when He judges that it is necessary to do so. After their difficult stay in Antioch and their dangerous journey, the Lord had prepared a surprise for the Apostles. The Lord informed Onesiphorus in a vision that Paul and Barnabas were going to Iconium.

Onesiphorus stood outside of the city looking at the travelers passing by in anticipation of meeting the Apostles. Suddenly, he saw two «strange» and exhausted individuals approaching. Their faces shone like a light in the dark. Onesiphorus was certain they were the Apostles the Lord had informed him of. He quickly approached them, venerated them and took them to his home. Paul could not forget the comfort Onesiphorus offered them. *«The Lord grant mercy to the household of Onesiphorus, for he often refreshed me...»* (2 Tim.1:16).

4.2. THE UPRISING OF THE IDOLATERS

News of Paul's and Barnabas' arrival spread among Jews and proselytes, who filled the synagogue. Paul's sermon was so dynamic, a large number of people believed in Christ (including Thekla, the Apostle's first female disciple who later became a martyr). However, fanatic Jews managed to turn the idolaters of the city against the Christians and the city was divided in two as a result (Acts 14:4).

Regardless of the events that had taken place, the Apostles remained in the city to reinforce the faith of the new Christians. The Jews continued to stir up the idolaters, who in turn continued their fight against the Christians of the city.

The rulers of the city sided with the Jews and they planned to kill the Apostles. Paul and Barnabas fled to Lystra, which was 40 km from Iconium. Once again, they made their way across the inhospitable plain. Things were about to get worse (Acts 14:3-7).

5
The Apostles in Lystra

The Greeks living in Lystra hellenized the residents of the city and the city had been devoted to the Gods Zeus and Hermes. The residents built a temple of Zeus which was near the city entrance. The annual religious festival in honor of Zeus was approaching.

The Apostles Paul and Barnabas stayed with a small Jewish family, one of the few which had not fallen within the realms of idolatry. The Apostles set up their «headquarters» at the home of Lois, Eunice and Timothy (who would become Paul's disciple) (2 Tim. 1:5).

5.1. DRAMATIC EVENTS

Preparations were being made for the annual religious festival. Hundreds of locals and visitors made their way to the temple of Zeus. There was truly a commotion. Paul's heart was broken as he watched the people gather. They seemed like sheep without a shepherd. He approached the city gate in order to preach to the people.

Until now, Paul had given his sermons in synagogues, where people gathered to hear words concerning God. However, this situation was completely different. The people had gathered to worship their god. They had not gathered to hear Paul speak. They looked at him with curiosity, for it was the first time they had seen a vessel of the Holy Spirit. They listened to him carefully[2].

There was a man who was born crippled in the crowd. Paul, seeing that the man had faith (he was listening carefully to his words) spoke out in a loud voice and said: «*Stand up straight on your feet!*» (Acts 14:10). The crippled

---

2 Cf. DANIEL ROBBS, *La Vie Quotidienne en Palestine au temps di Jesus*, Librairie Hachette 1961. Translated to Greek from French in 1988 by Dim. Papadima Press.

man leaped to his feat and walked! (Acts 14:8-11). Upon seeing the sight the crowd cried out in Lycaonian: *«"The gods have come down to us in the likeness of men!" And Barnabas they called Zeus, and Paul, Hermes, because he was the chief speaker»* (Acts 14:11-12). It was impossible for Paul to continue speaking because the atmosphere was so intense. Paul took Barnabas and they retreated to a small neighboring home. The festivities continued in the city streets and the residents were preparing to offer a sacrifice to Paul and Barnabas as a result of the miracle Paul had performed.

The residents of the city had already brought oxen to the city gates for the sacrifice. The idolater priest led the procession. The Apostles were in shock. They tore their clothes and ran among the crowd saying: *«Men, why are you doing these things? We also are men with the same nature as you, and preach to you that you should turn from these useless things to the living God, who made the heaven, the earth, the sea, and all things that are in them, who in bygone generations allowed all nations to walk in their own ways. Nevertheless He did not leave Himself without witness, in that He did good, gave us rain from heaven and fruitful seasons, filling our hearts with food and gladness»* (Acts 14:15-17). *«And with these sayings they could scarcely restrain the multitudes from sacrificing to them»* (Acts 14:18). Just as the Apostles thought they had managed to stop the sacrifice, things took a turn for the worse.

5.2. PAUL IS STONED

Sorcery was a mortal sin for the Judeans and anyone who performed magic or was linked to it in any way was worthy of being stoned to death. When Paul healed the crippled man, news of the event spread to Iconium and Antioch. The Jews (his adversaries) immediately labeled him a magician, which meant he was worthy of death (much to their satisfaction). It was a perfect opportunity to kill him!

The Judeans of Iconium made their way across the inhospitable plain to Lystra. They arrived after an 8-hour walk, ready to kill Paul. Others came from Antioch to take part (a five-day walk!)[3]. They met in Lystra and when they saw Paul, they violently seized him and dragged him like an animal out of the city. Then, they vehemently stoned him. They intensified their efforts (the number of stones being thrown increased) in order to make sure he was killed. When they were certain he was dead, they left him in the fields to be eaten by scavengers.

At sunset, Barnabas, who had been preaching in a nearby village, returned to Timothy's home. The entire household waited for Paul to return. When it got dark, they started to worry. A neighbor who happened to witness Paul's execution told them what had happened. Barnabas, Timothy, Lois, Eunice and Paul's disciples ran to the scene of the crime to retrieve his body (holy relic). The scene was horrific. Paul was full of blood and his body had been torn open. Just as they bent over to pick up his body, Paul rose! He got up and walked on his own! (Acts 14:19-20). They all returned to Timothy's home.

5.3. THE END OF THEIR STAY

At dawn, Paul and Barnabas left Lystra and went to Derbe, which was forty kilometers from Lystra. Derbe was by the border of Cilicia (Acts 14:20). This journey was different from the others because every step Paul took brought pain and suffering. His entire body was wounded. It can be assumed that Timothy helped him and probably carried him to Derbe on a stretcher together with Barnabas. When they arrived in Derbe, they most likely stayed at Gaius' home (who later be-

---

[3] Evil people refuse to do almost anything that is considered good, no matter how little effort is required. When it comes to doing evil, they go to great lengths to make sure they fulfil their goals (as was the case with the Judeans). On the other hand, those who wish to do good go to great lengths to fulfil their aims. When it comes to doing bad deeds, they simply refuse to do so.

came his disciple) (Acts 20:4). They cleaned his blood-filled body and tended to his wounds. They stood by his side and helped him until his recovery was complete.

Paul had scarcely recovered from his ordeal when he started preaching. He travelled to Antioch in Syria to continue preaching! However, he did not take the shortest route, which was through Cilicia. He went to Antioch (Syria) via Lystra, Iconium, and Antioch (Pisidia) in order to ordain ministers and reinforce the faith of the new Christians there, taking the same difficult and dangerous routes (Acts 14:21-22). «*We must through many tribulations enter the kingdom of God*», were his words to them (Acts 14:22). Prior to his departure (before Paul left his spiritual children in the hands the Lord), they fasted (which meant they did not eat anything) and prayed. This took place in every city Paul visited and preached in (Acts 14:23).

Paul returned to Antioch, along with Barnabas, where their difficult journey had begun approximately three years ago, after a long and exhausting journey. His epic journey lasted for a duration of approximately three years (45-48 AD). His thrilling journey spanned 1000 km on foot and 1000 km by sea. Paul «conquered» Salamis, Paphos, Antioch (Pisidia), Iconium, Lystra, Derbe and Perga.

6
Disputes Over the Law

A Greek proverb says: «*The soul leaves the body before its habits do*». Things that are deeply rooted in our souls (especially from childhood) are hard to eliminate from within. Judeans were raised with Judaism, which meant that circumcision and the Mosaic Law were «engraved» in their souls at a very early age. This was true even of Judeans who had become Christians!

The Jewish people were convinced that the Messiah came only for them. They believed that Gentiles who became Christians had to become members of Judaism first, which meant they had to be circumcised, follow Mosaic Law, abstain from sacrificial meat, and avoid contact with Gentiles (if they did not, they had to wash their hands and perform other rituals).

Jerusalem was the center of Judaism. Christians in Jerusalem were concerned about whether Christians in Antioch were following Mosaic Law. Some of the more rigid faithful decided to go to Antioch to see whether or not they were following the law or not. When they saw that Mosaic Law and more importantly, circumcision, were being overlooked, they said: «*Unless you are circumcised according to the custom of Moses, you cannot be saved*» (Acts 15:1). Paul and Barnabas did not agree with them and a heated dispute resulted. «*Therefore, when Paul and Barnabas had no small dispute with them, they determined that Paul and Barnabas and certain others of them should go up to Jerusalem, to the apostles and elders, about this question*» (Acts 15:2). Paul took a young man named Titus with him (who would later become his disciple of Crete (Gal. 2:1-5). «*So, being sent on their way by the church, they passed through Phoenicia and Samaria, describing the conversion of the Gentiles; and they caused great joy to all the brethren*» (Acts 15:3).

James, the brother of the Lord, who had been appointed bishop of Jerusalem because he was a relative of Christ, and the entire local Church warmly welcomed the representatives of the Church from Antioch (Acts 15:4), however, there was still a dispute between the two sides. When Paul and Barnabas informed them of the fact that God had opened the door of the faith to the Gentiles, «*some of the Pharisees who believed rose up, saying, "It is necessary to circumcise them, and to command them to keep the law of Moses"*» (Acts 15:5). They insisted that Titus be circumcised but Paul refused (Gal. 2:1-5).

6.1. THE APOSTOLIC SYNOD

The Apostolic Synod took place in 48 AD (Acts 15:6-35). Peter spoke first and was followed by Barnabas, Paul and James. They each presented their arguments concerning the matter (Acts 15:17-21). The decision reached was one which maintained a balance between the two sides. The Decree did not burden the Gentiles excessively nor did it disregard Mosaic Law. Specifically, it directed Gentile Christians to «*abstain from things offered to idols, from blood, from things strangled, and from sexual immorality*» (Acts 15:28-29).

The Synod informed the Church of Antioch of its decision in writing by sending Silas and Judas Barsabas to Antioch with Paul and Barnabas. The Decree concluded: «*If you keep yourselves from these, you will do well*» (Acts 15:22-29).

The Church in Antioch gathered together for the Divine Liturgy and the Decree was read. Silas explained the ambiguities of the Decree and answered questions (Acts 15:30-34). The dispute had been resolved. Judas Barsabas returned to Jerusalem, while Silas chose to stay in Antioch along with Paul and Barnabas, where they continued to preach the word of God (Acts 15:30).

7
Paul's Disagreement with Peter and Barnabas

Peter, Paul and Barnabas were human and just like any other person, they had different views on certain matters, regardless of the fact they were bearers of the Spirit.

The Apostle Peter was not obsessed with the things his fellow countrymen were concerning circumcision. He agreed with the Apostle Paul and Paul was aware of this. However, Peter did something which upset Paul greatly. Peter visited Antioch and was accompanied by John Mark (Barnabas' nephew). Peter had no problems in his interactions with the

Gentile Christians (he would sit with them and eat with them when they gathered together).

On the other hand, the faithful in Jerusalem could not take their minds off the Mosaic Law, so much so that they sent «spies» to Jerusalem to monitor Peter's behavior and actions. Peter realized what was taking place. He did not know what to do for Peter feared *«those who were of the circumcision»* (Gal. 2:12). As a result, he decided to side with his countrymen in Jerusalem. Barnabas was also misled as a result of Peter's actions! (Imagine how the others must have felt!).

Paul was also in Antioch at the time and could not bear Peter's «two-faced» stance. The Gentile Christians felt helpless and this distressed Paul greatly. He was afraid a schism would take place. Paul considered speaking out against Peter in public because Peter was committing «sin» in public. Paul, being a hierarch, had every right to speak out and so he did: *«If you, being a Jew, live in the manner of Gentiles and not as the Jews, why do you compel Gentiles to live as Jews?»* (Gal. 2:14). There are no written records of Peter's reply; therefore we do not know what he said[4].

It was now Barnabas' turn to have a disagreement with Paul: *«Then after some days Paul said to Barnabas, "Let us now go back and visit our brethren in every city where we have preached the word of the Lord, and see how they are doing". Now Barnabas was determined to take with them John called Mark. But Paul insisted that they should not take with them the one who had departed from them in Pamphylia, and had not gone with them to the work. Then the contention became so sharp that they parted from one another»* (Acts 15:36-37). Perhaps Barnabas believed that his nephew was now ready, after having followed the Apostle Peter. Paul refused to take him

---

[4] It is wrong to assume that Peter must have got upset upon hearing Paul's words. Peter listened to Paul with love and humility and loved him even more for his words, according ro Scripture: *«The wise, when rebuked, will love you»*. (Prov. 9:8), Paul did not reprimand Peter. He explained to him that what he was doing was wrong and he did so with love and humility.

with them. Barnabas insisted, however, Paul would not change his mind. «*Now Barnabas was determined to take with them John called Mark. But Paul insisted that they should not take with them the one who had departed from them in Pahmphylia, and had not gone with them to the work. Then the contention became so sharp that they parted form one another. And so Barnabas took Mark and sailed to Cyprus; but Paul chose Silas and departed, being commended by the bretheren to the grace of God*» (Acts 15:36-40).

Paul did not hold any grudges against Mark[5] (2 Tim. 4:11). The reason behind his decision was that he did not consider Mark a suitable travelling partner. He believed the journey was too difficult for Mark. Instead of taking a risk by taking Mark along, he preferred to risk parting with his childhood friend. He did everything he could to assure that his ministry «*not be blamed*» (2 Cor. 6:3).

Barnabas and Mark bid farewell to Paul. He in turn embraced them from the heart and wished them success in their holy ministry. Paul and Barnabas would not meet again. «*And so Barnabas took Mark and sailed to Cyprus*» (Acts 15:39). They went to Barnabas' hometown, Salamis where they preached the word of God.

Elymas was informed of the arrival of Barnabas and Mark and planned to seek revenge for being humiliated before the proconsul. Elymas stirred up the Jews and they killed Barnabas. Mark buried Barnabas' body in a Roman grave in Salamis. He placed a copy of the Gospel According to Matthew on his relic. In 489 AD during the reign of emperor Zenonos, Barnabas' tomb was discovered, as was his holy relic, together with the Gospel which was placed on it.

---

[5] We should recall that Paul suffered greatly in Antioch (Pisidia), Iconium, and Lystra. When he recovered, he immediately set out to preach in these cites again (Paul exhibited forbearance to the limit!). It was therefore certain that Paul's opinion of Mark was not out of contempt for him, for Paul did not show contempt for the above cities which caused him to suffer greatly (see Rom. 9:14).

8
The Apostles and The Holy Spirit

Peter, Paul and Barnabas possessed the Holy Spirit. Even so, they had disputes with each other. Why was this so?

The Apostles did indeed possess the Holy Spirit but they were not equal to the Holy Spirit. The Holy Spirit did take control of their minds. Never did they cease to possess free will. The Holy Spirit intervened whenever It saw fit or made revelations to them. For example, when Paul and his followers reached the border of Mysia in Asia Minor, they wanted to continue on the route which led to Bithynia, «*...but the Spirit did not permit them*» (Acts 16:7-8). When Paul contemplated leaving Corinth, the Lord Himself told him to stay: «*Do not be afraid but speak and do not keep silent*» (Acts 18:9). The Lord also told Paul to go to Jerusalem: «*And I went up by revelation...*» (Gal. 2:2). The Lord also told Paul to go to Macedonia and preach in a vision: «*Now after he had seen the vision, immediately we sought to go to Macedonia concluding that the Lord had called us to preach the gospel to them*» (Acts 16:10).

The Lord did not always intervene in the actions of the Apostles. «*The Apostles also made decisions on their own*» (St. John Chrysostom, Homily 49 on Acts). This means that when Paul did act on his own, he was subject to human error[6]. «*Therefore, when I was planning this, did I do it lightly?*» asked Paul in his epistle to the Corinthians (2 Cor. 2:17). Although Paul told the ministers in Ephesus that he would never see them again (Acts 20:15), and they broke out in tears (Acts 20:38), he did in fact see them again (2 Tim. 4:13-20). Paul sought for Titus in Troas (Acts 20:1-3) and Macedonia (2 Cor. 2:12-13) but could not find him (therefore the Holy Spirit did not guide him to Titus).

---

[6] St. John Chrysostom says the following concerning Saint Paul: «Again he discourses simply as a man and he does not enjoy the benefit of supernatural aid» (Homily 49:1 on Acts, P.G. 60:337).

Paul was aware of the fact that the Holy Spirit did not guide him on all occasions, which is why he told the Church in Jerusalem what he preached among the Gentiles just in case he «*had run, in vain*» (Gal. 2:2)[7]. The same is true of all the Apostles. «*The Apostles were not always under the influence of Divine Grace. God allowed them to deal with various matters on their own*» (St. John Chrysostom, Homily 21, 31:49 on Acts[8]).

When exactly did the Holy Spirit intervene in the lives of the Apostles? St. Basil tell us that «…the Spirit is ever present with those that are worthy, but works, as need requires…» (St. Basil the Great, On the Holy Spirit, Chapter 26, paragraph 61, P.G. 32:180). Even though the Holy Spirit was constantly present in the Apostles, it only intervened when It deemed necessary. «*Then Saul… filled with the Holy Spirit looked intently at him and said…*» (Acts 13:9). This is an indication that although Paul possessed the Holy Spirit, it intervened at that specific moment.

---

[7] Prominent teachers believe they are perfect at their work. They never stop to consider whether or not they may be at fault, which is why they never ask anyone their opinion of them. Paul on the other hand, did not believe he was perfect, even though Christ spoke to him in person! He was concerned about his strategy and asked for advice.

[8] Again Saint John Chrysostom says the following: «But observe, I pray you, how far it is from being the case that everything is done by (miraculous) grace, how on the contrary, God leaves many things to be managed for themselves by their own wisdom…» (Homily 21:1 on Acts, P.G. 60:164-165, 337.31:49).

Part Three

1
The Beginning of His Second Journey

Divine Providence was behind Silas' decision to remain in Antioch (Acts 15:34). He was to be Barnabas' successor. Being a prominent orator and a Roman citizen, he was the perfect person to accompany Paul on his apostolic mission. Paul summoned him to be his co-worker and to take the place of Barnabas (Acts 15:10). They began their apostolic mission after having received the blessing of the local Church.

The rejuvenated pair crossed Syria and eventually reached Cilicia (Acts 15:41), informing the masses of the decisions reached by the Synod in Jerusalem. They passed through the famous gate of Cilicia, a narrow path which crossed over a huge rock. They crossed the Taurus Mountains of Cilicia (which were nowhere near as difficult as the Taurus Mountains in Pamphylia) and eventually reached Derbe (Acts 16:1). Paul was extremely happy to see the brethren there and the Christians of the city were happy to see their spiritual father again. He carried out the Divine Liturgy, gave them Holy Communion, preached to them and ate with them. They discussed their problems with him and he gave them advice. He strengthened them with his presence and words. However, they felt empty because they wanted to see Barnabas also. He must have informed them that Barnabas had gone elsewhere.

Paul also returned to Lystra where he experienced much pain, to the home of Timothy (Acts 16:1). The family informed everyone of Paul's arrival and the Christians of the city, Paul's spiritual children, flocked to Timothy's home.

Paul's eyes were glued on Timothy, who was loved in Lystra and Iconium. Paul had definitely realized during his first visit that Timothy was suitable for Christ's mission and thus «recruited» him. Timothy bid farewell to his mother and grandmother and left them forever to serve Christ. Timothy was Paul's «compensation» for being stoned there the first time he visited the city (Acts 16:2-3).

Paul (the leader), Silas and Timothy made their way through the towns of Southern Galatia. They also passed through Antioch in Pisidia and informed the brethren of the decisions of the Synod in Jerusalem (Acts 16:45).

1.1. IN TROAS

It was now time to cultivate infertile lands that had not been cultivated before. Paul's desire was to preach the Gospel to the citizens of Rome (Rom. 15:32).

The Apostles had two routes to choose from. One went to the north into the depths of Asia Minor (to present day Ankara) while the other went west to the coast of Asia Minor, where the impressive Greek cities of Magnesia, Thyateira, Pergamos, Smyrna, and above all, Ephesus lay. There was certainly plenty of work to do there, however, the Holy Spirit said «no» and the Apostles took the route that headed north. They went through Phrygia, Galatia, Mysia and eventually reached Bithynia where Paul had the chance to rest a little and recover from his illness. The Holy Spirit, however, said «no» once again (the situation would truly have been disheartening for someone who wished to do his own will!). When they reached Troas, Luke the physician was waiting for them. The Holy Spirit has arranged for them to meet and from then on, Luke became Paul's co-worker and personal physician (Acts 16:6-10).

1.2. A MESSAGE FROM MACEDONIA

During Paul's stay in Troas, he saw a vision one night in which a Man from Macedonia pleaded him for help: «*Come over to Macedonia and help us*» (Acts 16:9). Paul, who was able to distinguish between a message from the above and Satan's deception, immediately told the others (Luke was now with them) and they set off on the first ship to Macedonia. «*Now after he had seen the vision, immediately we sought to go to Mace-*

donia, concluding that the Lord had called us to preach the gospel to them» (Acts 16:10).

Christ's four soldiers, with Paul at the helm, «invaded» Macedonia with the purpose of «conquering» it and bestowing it to Christ. The battle began in Philippi, the city built by Alexander the Great's father, Philip. (Philippi and Thessaloniki were the two most prominent cities of Macedonia, Philippi being the more prominent of the two).

The Apostle faced many difficulties in Macedonia. He was beaten, persecuted by the Romans and by his fellow countrymen (predominantly by his fellow countrymen!). He was so distressed by their demonic-like behavior he called the Jews «*dogs*» (Philip. 3:2). The following paragraphs summarize his experiences there.

2
In Philippi

Paul and his colleagues sailed to Samothrace, where they took another ship to Neapolis (modern day Kavala). They then set off on the two hour journey to Philippi, where they remained for a few days (Acts 16:11-13). They rented a small home where they made their plans for the future.

As was the custom, they first sought their fellow countrymen, however, there were so few Judeans in Philippi they did not even have a synagogue! They prayed on the banks of the Gaggiti River, which bordered the outskirts of the city. They gathered under maple trees along the river bank on Saturdays and worshipped God.

It was Saturday and the Apostles made their way to the river bank. They found a few women there, among who was a woman named Lydia from Thyatira in Asia Minor who traded purple. Paul spoke to her concerning Christ and she believed in Him! She was the first person in Macedonia (in Greece and in Europe) to believe in Him. She invited them to stay at her house: «*If you have judged me to be faithful to the Lord, come to my house and stay*». They did not accept her invitation at first but she persisted and they finally accepted: «*So, she persuaded us*» (Acts 16:11-15).

2.1. PAUL IS BEATEN AND IMPRISONED

The Apostles went to the Gaggiti River, together with Lydia and her family. On the way, they came across a slave girl who had a «*spirit of divination*». The girl was a fortune teller and she made profit for her masters (most people are interested in finding out about the future). The girl followed the Apostles saying: «*These men are the servants of the Most High God, who proclaim to us the way of salvation*» (Acts 16:17). Paul, who did not want the devil following him as if he were one his of his disciples, turned around and said: «*I command you in the name of Jesus Christ to come out of her*» (Acts 16:18). The spirit vanished, which meant that her masters' clients also «disappeared».

Her masters were enraged. They grabbed Paul and Silas and dragged them through the city streets in order to hand them over to the authorities. They said: «*These men, being Jews, exceedingly trouble our city; and they teach customs which are not lawful for us, being Romans, to receive or observe*» (Acts 16:20-21). The city authorities believed their lies and handed them over to be beaten. «*Then the multitude rose up together against them; and the magistrates tore off their clothes and commanded them to be beaten with rods. And when they had laid many stripes on them, they threw them into prison, commanding the jailer to keep them securely*» (Acts 16:22-23).

The prison guard led them to a dark, filthy basement cell in which their hands and feet were fastened in such a manner, every movement they made brought about pain. The cell door was secured by large wooden levers (Acts 16:24).

At night, Paul and Silas found the strength to pray and sing hymns, thus glorifying God, even though they had been beaten and could barely move. Their prayers were so intense, they could be heard by the other prisoners in neighboring cells (Acts 16:25).

Suddenly, a great earthquake shook the entire prison from its foundations. All the prison doors opened and the prisoners were freed! The prison guard thought the prisoners escaped and he took his sword in hand in order to kill himself. The Apostle Paul cried out in a loud voice: «*Do yourself no harm, for we are all here*» (Acts 16:28). The guard called for a lantern, closed the cell doors and bound the prisoners. He then fell before Paul and Silas and thanked them for saving his life. He took them out of their cell and said: «*Sirs, what must I do to be saved?*». They replied: «*Believe on the Lord Jesus Christ, and you will be saved, you and your household*». (Acts 16:26-34).

The guard and his family were all baptized. Outside it was dark, indoors, there was Light. The guard invited them to his home and set the table for them to eat. The family rejoiced for they were glad they had believed in Christ (Acts 16:26-34).

The great earthquake also awakened the conscience of the magistrates who unjustly imprisoned Paul and Silas. In the morning, they sent officers to the prison to release Paul and Silas. «*The magistrates have sent to let you go. Now therefore depart, and go in peace*». Paul replied: «*They have beaten us openly, uncondemned Romans, and have thrown us into prison. And now do they put us out secretly? No indeed! Let them come themselves and get us out*». The magistrates made their way to the city prison, apologized for what they had done and released them (Acts 16:36-39). «*So they went out of the prison and entered the house of Lydia; and when they had seen the brethren, they encouraged them and departed*» (Acts 16:40).

Paul saw it fit that one of them should remain in Philippi. He needed Luke with him because of his illness (and because his body was full of wounds). However, he judged that Luke was the most suitable person to stay behind. Christ's true servants place the benefit of the flock (Christians) above everything else. Paul departed together with Silas and Timothy.

There next stop was Thessaloniki and then Berea (the third judicial region of Macedonia). The situation in these cities was not any different. In fact, things would get worse!

3
The Apostles in Thessalonica and Berea

The Apostles (most likely) took the famous Egnatian Way in the spring of 50 AD and made their way to Thessalonica, which was a distance of 100 km from Philippi. Their wounds had not yet healed and their bodies were weak. They arrived in Amphipolis (the capital of Macedonia) after a two-day walk. After another two-day walk, they reached Apollonia and eventually they reached Thessalonica (Acts 17:1).

Thessalonica (previously named Thermes after Alexander the Great's sister) had the largest population (approximately 200,000) of all the cities in Macedonia. The Jewish population was large; therefore Thessalonica was considered the religious center of Macedonia. There were also many proselytes (who feared God) in Thessalonica.

When Paul arrived in Thessalonica, he went to his fellow countryman Jason, who was a merchant. Jason offered them Abraham-like hospitality. Lydia sent necessities from Philippi. In his epistle, Paul wrote: «*For even in Thessalonica you sent aid once and again for my necessities*». (Philip. 4:16) It is likely that Lydia was the one who suggested that Paul and his colleagues go to Jason.

The time had come for Paul to preach to the Thessalonians. He went to the city synagogue for three consecutive Saturdays and held discussions with his countrymen concerning the Messiah. He used Scripture to prove the Messiah had to suffer, be crucified and on the third day, rise from the dead. He argued that Christ suffered, was crucified and rose from the dead, which meant He was the Messiah, as foretold by Scripture.

Many Greek proselytes believed in Christ along with many women who belonged to the upper class. Many Jews also believed in Him (Acts 17:2-4). Paul also acquired two more co-workers in Thessalonica, Aristarchus and Secundus (Acts 20:4).

When the unfaithful Judeans saw the miracles that were taking place with the help of the Lord's grace, they decided to take action. They gathered together a group of «hooligans» who stirred up the entire city. They stood outside Jason's home in search of Paul and Silas. They wanted to hand the Apostles over to the angry mob in the city square in the center of Thessalonica. The Apostles managed to hide. The «hooligans» grabbed Jason and other Christians who were there and dragged them through the city streets to the authorities. They screamed: «*These who have turned the world upside down have come here too. Jason has harbored them, and these are all acting contrary to the decrees of Caesar, saying there is another king-Jesus*» (Acts 17:5-9). This was the worst thing a Roman citizen could be accused of. There was an uprising among the mob and the city authorities. Jason and the others were forced to pay a type of «bail» (a heavy fine) as a guarantee and were released.

Paul and Silas could no longer remain in Thessalonica. They waited for nightfall so they could leave without being seen. «*Then the brethren immediately sent Paul and Silas away by night to Berea*» (Acts 17:10). They avoided the Egnatian Way so as not to be seen and took another route to Berea in the dark with the help of lanterns. They reached Berea in the afternoon after walking all night. They hoped that they would not have to face the same ordeal in Berea, for they wished to return to Thessalonica as there was much work to be done there. The Apostle Paul tried to return to Thessalonica many times but to no avail (1 Thess. 2:18).

3.1. THE APOSTLES IN BEREA

Things went much more smoothly in Berea (for the time being). The Jews in Berea were more *«fair minded»* than the ones in Thessalonica (Acts 17:11). They studied Scripture and listened to Paul's teachings. Not only did they listen to his sermons but they were enchanted by them. Many people believed in Christ, including the wives of aristocrats, and many Greek women and men (Acts 17:11-12). In Berea, Sopater was also added to Paul's list of co-workers (Acts 20:4). When the Jews in Thessalonica were informed of Paul's presence in Berea and that his preaching was bearing much fruit, they made their way to Berea and stirred up the people!

The Christians of Berea sent Paul to Athens so he could escape the wrath of the Jews (Paul had been hoping to return to Thessalonica!). Paul was so exhausted, he collapsed on his way to the port where he left for Athens. Some of his spiritual children accompanied him to Athens. He commanded that Silas and Timothy stay in Berea.

When Paul and his spiritual children arrived in Athens, they found a Jewish family which agreed to accommodate Paul. Those who accompanied him returned to Berea (Acts, 17:15). Paul was alone in Athens!

4
In Athens

Although Athens did not resemble the Athens of the glorious years of Pericles, Socrates and Plato, it was nevertheless an impressive city. It possessed an impressive Academy, was home to numerous philosophers and there was the impressive Acropolis. In addition, Athens was the spiritual capital of the world (Jerusalem was the second and Ephesus was the third). The Parthenon was dedicated to the goddess Athena. One of the most revered monuments of the world was dedicated to a goddess! Athenian culture was not centered on people, it was centered on gods. Athena was not the only god they worshipped (there were some 3000!). The Athenians also worshipped the «Unknown God». The city was full of temples and altars, pillars, and statues of marble, bronze, silver and gold. No matter where you were, upon exiting a home, a temple was within sight. You were more likely to come across a temple before coming across a person when walking in Athens!

Imagine how Paul must have felt, being all alone in such a city! *«Now while Paul waited for them at Athens, his spirit was provoked within him when he saw that the city was given over to idols»* (Acts 17:16). He surely must have felt better when he was alone in the Arabian wilderness. Paul commanded that Silas and Timothy come to Athens as quickly as possible! (Acts 17:15). When Silas and Timothy arrived, Paul sent Silas to Berea and Timothy to Thessalonica. He preferred to remain on his own rather than deprive his spiritual children of their much-needed spiritual guides. Paul wanted them to be there so that they could provide them with encouragement when needed. *«Therefore, when we could no longer endure it, we thought it good to be left in Athens alone, and sent Timothy, our brother and minster of God, and our fellow laborer in the gospel of Christ, to establish you and encourage you concerning your faith, that no one should be shaken by these afflictions»* (1 Thess. 3:1-3).

4.1. PAUL'S DISCUSSIONS IN THE MARKET PLACE

The market place was in the center of the city. It abounded in temples, statues and shops. It resembled a city square. The Athenians would gather there along with foreigners and discuss current affairs. *«For all the Athenians and the foreigners who were there spent their time in nothing else but either to tell or to hear some new thing»* (Acts 17:21). Paul visited the market place daily and participated in discussions. On Saturdays, he would go to the synagogues and have discussions with Judeans and proselytes (Acts 17:17).

The Athenians, however, did not take to Paul's presence because he was short, bald, bull-legged, had a large nose, walked like a tortoise and spoke through his nose. His accent was also a problem. They found him repulsive. No one must have paid any attention to him in the beginning. It is highly likely that they mocked him. However, they could see the fruit of the Holy Spirit in his expression. They could sense his love and meekness (Gal. 5:22). His words were intelligent and he spoke of things they had never heard of before. The Athenians started to change slowly. They realized they had misjudged him. Paul suddenly became the center of attention. The city's philosophers were informed that this man spoke of things they had never heard of. The philosophers asked to come face to face with Paul. They proudly made their way to the market place together with their students in anticipation of meeting this man. The news spread and the market place was full of people.

The Epicureans spoke first. They told Paul that they were materialists and they believed in a God who was in isolation, a God who did not care about them. They told him that they did not believe in life after death, which is why they believed in seeking pleasure. The Stoics told him that they generally agreed with their colleagues (God was isolated from man and the soul was not immortal and did not continue to exist after death) but their goal was to attain a state of apathy with respect to joy and sorrow.

Both groups of philosophers believed that life ended at death. Paul, on the other hand, believed that life began after death. He spoke to them about Jesus and the Resurrection and explained that He gave meaning to life and death. He explained that death was the beginning of Life. It was as if he were saying to them: Believe in Christ and you will truly rejoice in life and death, for death leads to Life.

The philosophers were so obsessed with their thoughts they could not comprehend his words. «*"What does this babbler want to say?... He seems to be a proclaimer of foreign gods"*, *because he preached to them Jesus and the resurrection*» (Acts 17:18). They assumed that Jesus and the Resurrection were two separate foreign gods! Even so, something inside them told them that this man was not a common man. They considered Paul to be a divine being[1].

They took Paul to the Aeropagus, where respected elders of Athens judged matters concerning ethics, education and religion. The entire Aeropagus was known and respected by the entire world. Paul's words provoked so much thought in them they paid tribute to him by taking him to the Aeropagus so he could further explain his teachings. Paul was given a privilege offered only to chosen individuals.

5
Paul's Speech at the Areopagus[2]

෴

The head of the Areopagus said to Paul: «*May we know what this new doctrine is of which you speak? For you are bringing some strange things to our ears. Therefore, we want to know what these things mean*» (Acts 17:19-21). Paul stood in the middle. The members of the Areopagus were situated to his left and right while the philosophers stood before him, along with visitors who had gathered. Paul was ready to begin.

What was he going to say? Was he about to reveal his true feelings concerning their city (he was distressed by the sight of all the temples offered to idols)? He was not there to express his anger. He came to deliver the people from their ignorance. He was a fisher of men and he required bait for his

---

1 The Athenians believed that every so often, an «angel» with theological knowledge would appear before the people and teach them. Pythagoras, Embedocles, Chrysipus and Socrates were considered «angels». Now Paul appeared before them.
2 The Greek word *Areopagus* is derived from the words *pagus*, which means rock, and *Ares*, the ancient Greek god of war. It is literally translated «Ares' hill». The fact that trials took place on this hill (which often involved heated arguments) resulted in the hill being referred to as the «rock of war».

hook (there was no point in casting a hook without placing any bait on it). Paul did not express his true feelings to the Athenians. «*Men of Athens, I perceive that in all things you are very religious; for as I was passing through and considering the objects of your worship, I even found an altar with the inscription: "To the Unknown God". Therefore, the One whom you worship without knowing, Him I proclaim to you*» (Acts 17:22-24). Paul's words were the most effective approach to provoke thought and interest in them and win them over.

5.1. PART ONE

Paul tried to lead them from polytheism to the worship of monotheism, the worship of Jesus Christ, using their belief in the Unknown God to do so. Every word spoken by him was significant. There were many connotations in his speech. He inferred that the Unknown God was the creator of the world and all things in it: «*God who made the world and everything in it…*» (Acts 17:24). He did not tell them that the Unknown God was Jesus Christ. What he was insinuating was that because of the fact God created the world, the other gods they worshipped had done nothing and therefore should be considered non-existent. He told them that God «*is Lord of heaven and earth*» (Acts 17:24). God was not simply the creator of the world, He ruled the entire world. He gave a direct answer to the Epicurean and Stoic philosophers who believed that God had nothing to do with the world. Paul also told them that God «*does not dwell in temples made with hands*» (Acts 17:24). In other words, he was directly and politely telling them that their temples were useless and that the Unknown God had no need of them: «*Nor is He worshipped with men's hands, as though He needed anything, since He gives to all life, breath, and all things*» (Acts 17:25). The gods of the Athenians «required» servants and offerings (different foods etc.) Paul told the Athenians that the Unknwon God, on the other hand, provided for the people.

5.2. PART TWO

Paul's words were now more specific. He spoke to them of man's relationship with God (Jesus Christ): «*And He has made from one blood every nation of men to dwell on all the face of the earth…*» (Acts 17:26). He was telling them that all the people of the earth were brothers and that they all had a common ancestor, Adam, and the same God. The ancient Greeks considered people who did not worship their gods barbarians. Paul told the Athenians that God determined «*the boundaries of their dwellings so that they should seek the Lord, in the hope that they might grope for Him and find Him…*» (Acts 17:27). Paul used the word «Lord», not «God», in reference to Jesus Christ. He indirectly told them they were in the darkness of polytheism and were searching for the truth. He also told them they were not far from finding Him: «*He is not far from each one of us*» (Acts 17:27). Paul attempted to provoke thought in them for he hoped they would start searching for God. Paul used a verse from one of their poets to convince them to do so: «*As also some of your own poets have said, "For we are also His offspring"*» (Acts 17:28). In an effort to prevent them from misinterpreting the nature of Divinity, he said: «*Therefore, since we are the offspring of God, we ought not to think that the divine Nature is like gold or silver or stone, something shaped by art and man's devising*» (Acts 17:29).

5.3. PART THREE

The purpose behind Paul's visit to Athens was to preach Jesus Christ's Crucifixion and Resurrection. Until now, Paul had not spoken a word about Christ. He was slowly paving the way. The time for him to speak about Jesus was drawing near.

The Athenians listened to Paul quietly. They waited to see where his speech would lead to. He continued: «*Truly, these times of ignorance God overlooked, but now commands all men everywhere to repent…*» (Acts 17:30). Paul was telling them that God forgave them because they did not know Him but now that they had heard of him, He wanted them to repent.

«…He has appointed a day on which He will judge the world in righteousness by the Man whom He has ordained» (Acts 17:31). Paul referred to Christ as a «Man», the reason being that the Athenians believed in the existence of «divine people». When they heard that a «Man» would be the judge of the world, they listened carefully. Paul continued: *«He has given assurance of this to all by raising Him from the dead»* (Acts 17:31).

Just as he was preparing to mention the name of Jesus Christ, the Athenians' reaction hurt him immensely and he could no longer speak. *«And when they heard of the resurrection of the dead, some mocked, while others said, "We will hear you again on this matter"»* (Acts 17:32). Paul could not bear hearing them laugh at Christ and it broke him in two. He left for Corinth without saying a word! He never returned to Athens (not even on his third journey), nor did he ever mention the city in his epistles, which is an indication of how seriously he was affected by their response. It is safe to say that this was the only time he was discouraged during his turbulent and lengthy apostolic mission.

6
Conclusion

If someone who possessed *«zeal for God, but not according to knowledge»* (Rom. 10:2) had heard Paul's words at the Areopagus, he would have been outraged. One could conclude that Paul made two unforgiveable «mistakes» in his speech at the Areopagus.

1st: Paul did not mention Christ in his speech. When he indirectly referred to Him, he called Him a «Man» (as Jehovah's witnesses do). Paul's zeal for God (he was not a fanatic) told him that the time had not come to reveal to the Athenians that Christ was God. In other words, Paul would definitely have mentioned His name and called Him the True God had he continued to speak. He approached the matter slowly but did not manage to complete his speech. There was no way that Paul would not have mentioned Christ, the Savior of the world.

2nd: When the Athenians mocked Paul, he should have stayed and persisted in his words before leaving. He should have left only if they continued mocking his words (after scolding them). Paul's zeal for God told him that people who mock and laugh at the divine are not worthy of hearing the holy name of Christ, therefore he should get up and leave.

6.1. THE ATHENIANS HAD A PROBLEM

Scripture tells us: «*The beginning of pride is when one departeth from God*» (Wisdom 10:12). People who are distant from Jesus Christ are inundated with pride. People who wish to return to Christ must humble themselves. The Athenians were proud of their civilization, their philosophers and their level of education. However, the Apostle Paul tells us: «*Knowledge puffs up*» (1 Cor. 8:1). The Athenians' conceit was an obstacle which blocked their way to the Truth. They sought to be freed of their belief in polytheism (they sought Christ) but in order to do so, they had to humble themselves in order to believe in Him (they did not which is why they did not believe in Him).

The Athenians worshipped 3,000 gods. What else could Paul offer them? The truth is they were not fulfilled by their beliefs, which is why they asked Paul to speak in the first place. The Athenians may have worshipped many gods but in fact, they did not worship anything because there is only One True God. Regardless of the number of gods one worships, there is no fulfillment because they are false. The Athenians were without God, which is why they were interested in discovering God through Paul.

Paul's teachings provoked so much thought in the Athenians they led him to the Areopagus to speak (even though they found his appearance and accent repulsive). Paul told them exactly what they wanted to hear but they had a problem «*and their foolish hearts were darkened*» (Rom. 1:21).

On the other hand, some Athenians were overwhelmed by Paul's words, so much so they denied their faith and believed in Jesus Christ. Dionysius the Areopagite[3], and a woman named Damaris were two of these people (Acts 17:33).

Why did this group of people believe while the others mocked Paul? Did they possess something different from the others? They were not necessarily more intelligent than the others but they were good-willed. Paul inferred that there was light in each person which was there to help people find the Lord. Dionysius and Damaris intensified the light within and their minds and souls were enlightened and they saw the Truth. «*For to know the law is of a sound mind*» (Prov. 9:10). On the other hand, those who did not believe tried to kindle their flame within but it eventually went out. The Athenians preferred to worship the Unknown God, not Jesus Christ. They preferred to worship their 3,000 gods (who they probably didn't even know) instead of Jesus Christ, who was crucified and rose from the dead for their salvation!

Belief in Christ is not a simple matter. It requires strength. One must toil to believe, which is why Christ said to the father of the sick child: «*If you can believe, all things are possible…*» (Mark 9:23). Christ did not ask the child's father if he believed. He asked him if he was capable of believing!

---

[3] According to the book Μέγας Συναξαριστής τῆς Ὀρθοδόξου Ἐκκλησίας, Ἀθῆναι 2001, ἔκδοσις Πέμπτη, τόμος 100ς σελ. 73, he was the first bishop (overseer) of Athens and a martyr. He was put to death by decapitation. When his head was cut off, he picked it up, walked a distance of two miles and handed it a Christian woman named Katoula. The event shocked the arrogant Athenians but it was also a lesson to them. It may sound unlikely but who would have dared to mention the event if it were not true? Who would have believed the event if only one person had witnessed it? The fact that the event was recorded in history is evidence that numerous people witnessed it. If this were not the case, who would have dared to tell such a tale?

7
Paul in Corinth

The Jewish population in Rome often troubled the Christians of the city, causing conflict in Rome. The emperor Claudius wanted to put an end to this and commanded the Jews to leave Rome. Many of them ended up in Corinth. As a result, Corinth had a large Jewish population. Priscilla and Aquila of Pontus were a Jewish Christian couple who moved to Corinth. Aquila was a tentmaker who was born in Pontus, migrated to Rome and now moved to Corinth (Acts 18:1-5).

Corinth was the capital of Achaia. It had a population of approximately 200,000 and possessed an important merchant port. Athens was the center of education and studies while Corinth was a city of trade. Thousands of merchants, sailors and foreigners visited the city via its port. The city was reminiscent of a brothel. There were more than 1,000 brothels in Corinth. People who visited the city were in danger of being overtaken by immorality.

When the Apostle Paul saw what the situation in Corinth was like, he wondered whether it was worth preaching there or not. He was still in a state of grief from his experience in Athens. Everything seemed gloomy. God, who continuously followed Paul, judged that He needed to intervene in order to encourage His servant. He appeared to him in the middle of the night and said: «*Do not be afraid, but speak, and do not keep silent; for I am with you, and no one will attack you to hurt you; for I have many people in this city*» (Acts 18:9-11). Paul stayed in Corinth for approximately a year and a half.

In the meantime, Timothy and Silas arrived from Thessalonica and Berea respectively. The news they brought (especially from Thessalonica) was good. Paul took courage seeing that his efforts were not in vain. He wrote to the Thessalonians. «*But now that Timothy has come to us from you, and brought us good news of your faith and love, and that you always have good remembrance of us, greatly desiring to see us»* (1 Thess. 3:6). He told them that he and the others had taken courage from them and that their faith had been reinforced because they were steady and remained close to the Lord. *«For now we live, if you stand fast in the Lord»* (1 Thess. 3:8). *«For this reason we also thank God witout ceasing, because when you received the word of God which you heard from us, you welcomed it not as the word of men, but as it is in truth, the word of God, which also effectively works in you who believe. For you, brethren, became imitators of the churches of God which are in Judea (…) for you also suffered the same things from your own countrymen, just as they did from the Judeans, who killed both the Lord Jesus and their own prophets…»* (1 Thess. 2:13-15).

Paul was now in the right frame of mind to preach. He went to the city synagogue every Saturday and held discussions with the Jews and proselytes in an effort to convince them that Jesus, who was crucified, buried and rose from the dead, was the Messiah they were awaiting. Unfortunately, Paul could not convince them. They blasphemed when they heard his words (Acts 18:6) even though they were in a place of prayer and Scripture! Until now, Paul bore everything he had faced with unprecedented forbearance. This time, things were different. He shook the dust off his clothes to show them that he was not responsible for their unwillingness to be saved: *«Your blood be upon your own heads; I am clean. From now on I will go to the Gentiles»* (Acts 18:6).

He left the synagogue and went to the house of Justus who lived next to the synagogue (Acts 18:7). There was definitely a purpose behind his decision to stay with Justus. Because of the fact that Justus lived next to the synagogue, many of the people would pass by his home to visit Paul on their way to and from the synagogue. Paul taught them concerning Christ. Crispus, the ruler of the synagogue, and his family believed in Christ! In Corinth, Paul himself baptized the people who accepted his words (his co-workers were the ones who usually baptized the people) (1Cor. 1:14-15). It was the perfect way to «mislead» the corrupt Corinthians into believing.

The Lord promised Paul that no one would attack him and kill him (Acts 18:10). Paul, therefore, had peace of mind. However, it seemed that the Lord did not exactly keep His word. The Lord permitted for His chosen servant Paul to suffer once again (surely He had His purpose).

The unfaithful Judeans grabbed him and took him to the proconsul Gallio, the brother of Seneca. They were certain the proconsul would convict Paul: «*This fellow persuades men to worship God contrary to the law*» (Acts 18:12-14). He was about to defend himself when Gallio spoke: «*If it were a matter of wrong-doing or wicked crimes, O Jews, there would be reason why I should bear with you. But if it is a question of words and names and your own law, look to it yourselves...*» (Acts 18:15-16).

The Jews froze but did not give up. Together with Sosthenes, the synagogue ruler, they insisted that Paul be convicted. Gallio told them to leave but they would not depart.

A curious crowd of Greeks had gathered to see what was happening. When they saw Sosthenes' outrage, they could no longer tolerate the situation. They seized him and beat him. Gallio acted as if nothing was happening (Acts 18:15-22). The Lord had truly come to Paul's defense!

7.1. PAUL LEAVES CORINTH

During difficult times, Jewish people refrained from cutting their hair and abstained from alcohol for a month. They then cut their hair and burnt it at the altar of the temple of Jerusalem[4]. Paul took this same vow when he was in Corinth. He arranged to sail to Antioch (Syria) so he could fulfill his vow. He had his hair cut at Cenchera and then planned to go

---

4 What was the reason behind this? Vows are holy and whatever has been offered to God must not be discarded as waste. Paul's body was dedicated to God, including his head, which is why the Almighty Lord does not permit members of the clergy to cut their hair (Lev. 19:27, 21:5-10).

to Jerusalem to burn his hair at the temple. Paul was to embark on such a lengthy journey for the purpose of burning his hair at the temple of Jerusalem! «*Then he took leave of the brethren and sailed for Syria, and Priscilla and Aquila were with him*» (Acts 18:18-19).

Paul's first stop, albeit frequent, was Ephesus, the capital of the coast of Asia Minor. He went to the synagogue on Saturday to preach to his fellow countrymen. They were so enchanted by his preaching, they asked him to stay longer. «*I must by all means keep this coming feast in Jerusalem; but I will return again to you*» (Acts 18:21).

Paul left Aquila and Priscilla behind and sailed to Caesarea with Silas and Timothy. «*And when he had landed at Caesarea, and gone up* (to Jerusalem) *and greeted the Church, he went down to Antioch*» (Acts 18:12).

Having fulfilled his vow in Jerusalem, he went to Antioch in Syria (Acts 18:22-23) where he met up again with the Apostle Peter and offered him his worthy co-worker Silas. Silas thus became the Apostle Peter's disciple (1 Peter 5:12). Paul sent Timothy to Corinth to «reacquaint» the Corinthians with the gospel (1 Cor. 4:17). Paul's second journey (some 3,000 km) had come to an end (49-52 AD).

Part Four

1
The «Overtaking» of Ephesus

Paul set off on his third journey. The first stop was Ephesus. He had told them that he would return during his first visit to Ephesus (Acts 18:21). Paul could have gone to Seleucia and sailed to Ephesus but he chose to go via Galatia. He visited the Churches in Derbe, Lystra, Iconium and Antioch and strengthened them. He bid them farewell, crossed the rugged mountain ranges of Asia Minor and reached Ephesus (Acts 19:1).

1.1. EPHESUS

Ephesus, the capital of Asia Minor, was the third religious capital of the world. It had a population of approximately 200,000. The entire region was made up of a total of 500 cities and towns. Ephesus was also the epicenter of sorcery and pagan worship (the goddess Artemis or Diana). The pagan temple was located in the center of the city square and a huge statue of Artemis stood before it. The residents believed Zeus had sent the statue from the heavens. The temple was so vast it was considered one of the seven wonders of the world. The temple roof was supported by 127 Ionic pillars which had special designs at their base. The altar was decorated with the works of famous artists (Phidias, Praxiteles, Polycleitus, etc).

A special (holy) street, which was two kilometers in length, led to the temple. Ships continuously brought visitors from all over the world, especially in May when the festival of Artemis took place. The visitors would walk along the path together with priests, singers, musicians and policemen and make their way to the temple. Silversmiths made replicas of the temple which they sold to visitors as souvenirs. Ephesus was definitely a challenge for the Apostle Paul. *«But I will tarry in Ephesus until Pentecost. For a great and effective door has opened to me, and there are many adversaries»* (1Cor. 16:8-9), wrote Paul to the Corinthians.

1.2. EPHESUS IS «OVERTAKEN»

In Ephesus, Paul wished to accomplish what he could not accomplish in Athens. He wished to convert the city from a center of sorcery and idolatry to a Christian center and he was successful. He was so well organized, he managed to visit the entire region surrounding Ephesus during his two-year stay there. Ephesus was not the only city to accept the word. The city of Colosse accepted the word (with the help of the Greek minister Epaphras, see Col. 1:7), along with Laodicea and Hierapolis (Col. 4:12). Demetrius, the idolater silversmith said to his fellow craftsmen: *«Moreover you see and hear that not only at Ephesus, but throughout almost all Asia, this Paul has persuaded and turned away many people, saying that they are not gods which are made with hands»*. (Acts 19:26) Paul's presence in Ephesus caused an «earthquake» and «tidal wave» that washed away sorcery and idolatry. Let us examine how this happened (Acts 19:11-20).

Initially, Paul attempted to persuade the idolaters in Ephesus with his sermons. He was not successful, though. In order to convince them, he employed the use of «effects» (miracles). *«Now God worked unusual miracles by the hands of Paul, so that even handkerchiefs or aprons were brought from his body to the sick, and the diseases left them and the evil spirits went out of them»* (Acts 19:11). The following is an example of one such miracle.

During Paul's stay in Ephesus, the sons of the Jewish chief priest Sceva, who were exorcists, were in Ephesus. They made quite a profit exorcising demons from people. When they heard that Paul was exorcising demons in the name of Christ, they imitated him in an attempt to increase their earnings. They were not aware of the fact that the name of Christ cleansed those who believed Him to be God and the Savior of the world, and lived according to His teachings. Nor did they know that using His name for evil purposes was «dangerous». They stayed in a home where they waited for clients to come.

Their first client arrived. The exorcists said: «*We exorcise you by the Jesus whom Paul preaches*» (Acts 19:13). The evil spirit replied: «*Jesus I know, and Paul I know; but who are you?*» (Acts 19:15). Instead of leaving the possessed man, the evil spirit attacked them and knocked them to the floor. The spirit stripped them of their clothing, beat them and the exorcists fled from the home!

News of the event spread throughout Ephesus and the name of Christ was glorified (Acts 19:15-17). The devil was unable to accommodate his «servants». He could not be trusted. The devil could not withstand hearing the name of Jesus Christ and this proves how weak he is compared to Christ.

Many people were overcome with fear and thus glorified the name of Christ. Many people who were involved in sorcery confessed their association with sorcery. They brought their books with them and burned them in front of everyone. A huge pile of books (which were estimated to cost 50,000 pieces of silver!) was burned and the raging fire could be seen everywhere in Ephesus! (Acts 19:18-20).

2

The Public Uprising in Ephesus

When Paul set foot in Ephesus in 54 AD, he preached in the synagogue for three months (May, June and July) in an effort to convince the Ephesians that Christ was the Messiah. When Paul saw that some of his countrymen were twisting his words and teachings, he took his co-workers, left the synagogue and they never set foot there again (Acts 19:9). Paul rented a large hall (the school of Tyrannus) and preached there for five hours (from 11:30 am to 4:30 pm) every day for two years. He worked the remaining hours of the day in order to pay for rent and expenses (he was not alone). Many visitors who visited the city went to the school of Tyrannus to listen to Paul preach. Those who believed in Christ returned to their homelands and passed on the word of salvation to their homes, relatives and friends. The word of the Lord was spreading all over Asia (Acts 19:9-10). Two years had passed since the Apostle Paul's arrival in Ephesus. Things were getting difficult. He had no food to eat, water to drink nor clothes to wear. The idolaters reviled him. He admitted the difficult situation he was facing in his epistle to the Corinthians: «*For I think that God has displayed us, the apostles, last, as men condemned to death… To the present hour we both hunger and thirst, and we are poorly clothed, and beaten, and homeless. And we labor working with our hands… We have been made as the filth of the world, the offscouring of all things until now*» (1 Cor. 4:9-14).

Paul was considering leaving Ephesus and going to Macedonia (to Philippi, Thessalonica, and Berea), Corinth (no mention of Athens), Jerusalem, Rome and then Spain (Rom. 15:28). He sent Timothy and Erastus to Macedonia while he remained in Ephesus for a while (Acts 19:21-23). Perhaps he remained in Ephesus for the festival of Artemis, for May was approaching and a sea of people were to flock there for the festivities. Paul, being a fisher of men, was anticipating a good catch; however, a «hurricane» ruined his plans…

2.1. THE PUBLIC UPRISING

«*And about that time there arose a great commotion about the Way*» (Acts 19:23). «*I have fought with beasts at Ephesus*», wrote Paul (1 Cor. 15:32). «*For we do not want you to be ignorant, brethren, of our trouble which came to us in Asia: that we were burdened beyond measure, above strength, so that we despaired even of life. Yes, we had the sentence of death in ourselves, that we should not trust in ourselves but in God who raises the dead, who delivered us from so great a death…*» (2 Cor. 1:8-10).

What exactly happened? Demetrius, the idolater silversmith who made silver replicas of the temple of Artemis, sold many of his works to visitors. Paul's preaching brought about a decline in sales and he was in danger of going out of business. He called his fellow craftsmen together and he caused an uprising (he mixed religion with business). Demetrius and his employees went on the counter-attack. «*So not only is this trade of ours in danger of falling into disrepute, but also the temple of the great goddess Diana may be despised and her magnificence destroyed, whom all Asia and the world worship*» (Acts 19:25-27). When his men heard this, they were enraged and cried out: «*Great is Diana of the Ephesians!*» (Acts 19:28). Their shouting and stomping could be heard everywhere in the city! They ran to the home of Aquila in search of Paul. They wanted to seize him and throw him to the beasts to be devoured. They found Paul's co-workers Gaius and Aristarchus instead. They seized them and took them to the coliseum (Acts 19:29).

Paul, who was preaching in the school of Tyrannus, heard the news. He was about to interrupt his sermon and go to the theatre but the Christians would not allow him to go so as not to make an already difficult situation worse. Some officials who were friends of Paul also sent him a message telling him not to go to the theatre (Acts 19:30-31). The «lion» was now locked up in a cage. He was concerned about Gaius and Aristarchus. He was unaware of their condition and was anxious to find out what had happened.

Things were going from bad to worse. An uprising of the people followed. The entire city was revolting! Everyone gathered at the theatre. Some climbed trees while others went to the hillside which faced the sea shore to see what was happening.

The people were enraged with the Jews of the city. They dragged them to the theatre also. The Jews sent Alexander, Paul's foremost adversary, to the front to explain to the Ephesians that they had nothing to do with the Apostle Paul. Alexander motioned to the crowd to quieten down. When they saw that a Jew was about to speak, they started crying out:

«*Great is Diana of the Ephesians*» (Acts 19:32-34). They would not let Alexander speak a word.

The city clerk tried to quieten down the people but to no avail. He finally managed to do so after two hours! He was an intelligent and responsible man. He spoke with such intelligence and realism that he managed to convince the crowd to stop. «*Men of Ephesus, what man is there who does not know that the city of the Ephesians is temple guardian of the great goddess Diana, and of the image which fell down from Zeus? Therefore since these things cannot be denied, you ought to be quiet and do nothing rashly. For you have brought these men here who are neither robbers of temples nor blasphemers of your goddess. Therefore, if Demetrius and his fellow craftsmen have a case against anyone, the courts are open and there are proconsuls. Let them bring charges against one another. But if you have any other inquiry to make, it shall be determined in the lawful assembly. For we are in danger of being called in question for today's uproar, there being no reason which we may give to account for this disorderly gathering*» (Acts 19:35-41). The crowd dispersed at the conclusion of his speech.

3
The Epistles from Ephesus

While Paul was in Ephesus for two years, he was informed of what was taking place in the local Churches he had established by messengers. Unfortunately, the news from Galatia and Corinth was not good, which is why he sent epistles to the Churches there.

3.1. THE EPISTLE TO THE GALATIANS

When the shepherd is absent, wolves come in to devour the flock. As soon as Paul left Galatia for Ephesus, the Church fell into a state of turmoil. False apostles had gone to Galatia from Jerusalem and they presented fake epistles which they said were from James. Their aim was to slander Paul. They told the Christians in Galatia that Paul was guilty of overlooking the Mosaic Law and that he was not a true apostle of Christ like Peter and the others (who followed Christ and lived with Him). These false apostles spread their lies everywhere in Galatia. They attended Divine Liturgies with false piety and preached their lies. They even went to the homes of Christians to criticize Paul. As a result, the people were divided and a dispute arose between both sides (Gal. 5:15). Galatia was «on fire».

Paul heard about what had taken place in Galatia and sent a «bitter» epistle which he wrote himself in which he explained that he was a true Apostle of Christ and that with the coming of Christ, the law was now void (Gal. 6:15).

3.1.1. A TRUE APOSTLE

I marvel that you are turning away so soon from Him who called you in the grace of Christ, to a different gospel, which is not another; but there are some who trouble you and want to pervert the gospel of Christ. But even if we, or an angel from heaven, preach any other gospel to you than what we have preached to you, let him be accursed. As we have said before, so now I say again, if anyone preaches any other gospel to you than what you have received, let him be accursed. For do I now persuade men or God? Or do I seek to please men? For if I still pleased men, I would not be a bondservant of Christ. But I make known to you, brethren, that the gospel which was preached by me is not according to man. For I neither received it from man, nor was I taught it, but it came through the revelation of Jesus Christ (Gal. 1:6-12).

3.1.2. CHRIST AND THE MOSAIC LAW

But before faith came, we were kept under guard by the law, kept for the faith which would afterward be revealed. Therefore the law was our tutor to bring us to Christ, that we might be justified by faith. But after faith has come, we are no longer under a tutor. For you are all sons of God through faith in Christ Jesus. For as many of you as were baptized into Christ have put on Christ (Gal. 3:23-27).

3.2. THE FIRST EPISTLE TO THE CORINTHIANS

The Church in Corinth was being plagued by sexual immorality, slander against the Apostle Paul, elders who were playing the role of spiritual father, and division. When Paul heard the news, he thought of sending Apollos to Corinth, who had already preached in Corinth and had returned to Ephesus (together with Sosthenes, the former ruler of the synagogue in Corinth who had become a Christian) (1Cor. 1:1). Apollos was capable of bringing peace to the Church, however, Apollos wanted nothing to do with Corinth. Paul pleaded with him but to no avail (1Cor. 16:12). Paul, who was crushed when he heard what was taking place in Corinth, dictated an epistle to Sosthenes, (the first epistle to the Corinthians) (1 Cor. 1:1). Titus personally delivered the epistle to Corinth. The following is a summary of the epistle:

3.2.1. *THE «ELDERS»*

Some people in Corinth were certain that Paul would not return. As a result, they played the role of spiritual leader or elder. The Church was in turmoil. Paul wrote to them: «*Now some are puffed up, as though I were not coming to you. But I will come to you shortly, if the Lord wills, and I will know, not the word of those who are puffed up, but the power. For the kingdom of God is not in word but in power. What do you want? Shall I come to you with a rod, or in love and a spirit of gentleness?*» (1 Cor. 4:18-21).

«*I do not write these things to shame you, but as my beloved children I warn you. For though you might have ten thousand instructors in Christ, yet you do not have any father; for in Christ Jesus I have begotten you through the gospel. Therefore I urge you, imitate me. For this reason I have sent Timothy to you, who is my beloved and faithful son in the Lord, who will remind you of my ways in Christ, as I teach everywhere in every church»* (1 Cor. 4:14-17).

3.2.2. FACTIONS

Christians from Chloe's household informed Paul that there were contentions between the Christians in Corinth. More specifically, four factions had formed (1 Cor. 1:11)[1]. Each faction had its leader (false apostle). Furthermore, the factions were at odds with each other. Paul wrote: *«Who then is Paul, and who is Apollos, but ministers through whom you believed, as the Lord gave to each one? I planted, Apollos watered but God gave the increase. So then neither he who plants is anything, nor he who waters, but God who gives the increase. Now he who plants and he who waters are one, and each one will receive his own reward according to his own labor. For we are God's fellow workers; you are God's field, you are God's building. According to the grace of God which was given to me, as a wise master builder I have laid the foundation, and another builds on it. But let each one take heed how he builds on it. For no other foundation can anyone lay than that which is laid, which is Jesus Christ. Now if anyone builds on this foundation… each one's work will become clear»* (1 Cor. 3:5-13).

3.2.3. A TRUE APOSTLE

Paul's adversaries pointed out that he was not one of the twelve Apostles and therefore claimed that he did not «belong». Weaker Christians were affected by these words upon hearing them. Paul replied: *«Am I not an apostle? Am I not free? Have I not seen Jesus Christ our Lord? Are you not my work in the Lord? If I am not an apostle to others, yet doubtless I am to you, for you are the seal of my apostleship in the Lord»* (1 Cor. 9:1-2).

---

1 The first faction supported Apollos and rejected Paul because he was not one of Christ's twelve Apostles. The second favored Peter over Paul. The third supported Paul while the fourth faction claimed that they discovered Christ on their own and so belonged to Him (2 Cor. 11:5).

Paul went further. The destitute Apostles, being shepherds of the people, had the right to be supported and served by their flock (the local Churches). The Apostle Peter and the others were supported by Christians. They were also accompanied by a woman who served them. Paul did not wish to do the same, although he had the right to. He used this fact as an argument to prove that he was just as worthy as the twelve Apostles, and even more so! He wrote: «*My defense to those who examine me is this: Do we have no right to eat and drink? Do we have no right to take along a believing wife, as do also the other apostles, the brothers of the Lord, and Cephas? Or is it Barnabas and I who have no right to refrain from working? Who ever goes to war at his own expense? Who plants a vineyard and does not eat of its fruit? Or who tends a flock and does not drink of the milk of the flock? Do I say these things as a mere man? Or does not the law say the same also? For it is written in the law of Moses, "You shall not muzzle an ox while it treads out the grain". Is it oxen God is concerned about? Or does He say it altogether for our sakes? For our sakes, no doubt, this is written, that he who plows should plow in hope, and he who threshes in hope should be partaker of his hope. If we have sown spiritual things for you, is it a great thing if we reap your material things? If others are partakers of this right over you, are we not even more? Nevertheless we have not used this right, but endure all things lest we hinder the gospel of Christ*» (1 Cor. 9:3-12).

3.2.4. CONCERNING SEXUAL IMMORALITY

«*It is actually reported that there is sexual immorality among you, and such sexual immorality as is not even named among the Gentiles-that a man has his father's wife! And you are puffed up and have not rather mourned, that he who has done this deed might be taken away from among you. For I indeed, as absent in body but present in spirit, have already judged (as though I were present) him who has so done this deed*» (1 Cor. 5:1-3). *All things are lawful for me but all things are not helpful. All things are lawful for me but I will not be brought under the power of any... Now the body is not for sexual immorality but for the Lord, and the Lord for the body. Do you not know that your bodies are members of Christ? Shall I then take the members of Christ and make them members of a harlot? Certainly not!... Or do you not know that your body is a temple of the Holy Spirit who is in you, whom you have from God, and you are not your own? (1 Cor. 6:12-20). Do you not know that the unrighteous will not inherit the kingdom of God? Do not be deceived. Neither fornicators... nor adulterers, nor homosexuals, nor sodomites... will inherit the kingdom of God* (1 Cor. 6:9-10).

3.2.5. CONCERNING SPOUSES

While Paul was writing his first epistle to the Corinthians, he received a message from certain Christians of Corinth who asked him for advice concerning marital relations. He answered that marriage existed in order to protect people from fornication. More specifically: «*Now concerning the things of which you wrote to me: It is good for a man not to touch a woman. Nevertheless, because of sexual immorality, let each man have his own wife, and let each woman have her own husband... Do not deprive one another except with consent for a time, that you may give yourselves to fasting and prayer; and come together again so that Satan does not tempt you because of your lack of self-control. But I say this as a concession not as a commandment. For I wish that all men were even as I myself... but if they cannot exercise self-control, let them marry. For it is better to marry than to burn with passion*» (1 Cor. 7:1-10).

4
News from Corinth

Titus delivered the first epistle to the Corinthians and returned to Ephesus in order to report to Paul. He informed Paul that things were getting worse in Corinth. Paul sent a second epistle to Corinth, which was also personally delivered by Titus.

His second epistle was much harsher than the first (there are no records of this epistle today).

Upon returning from Corinth after his second journey, Titus was to meet Paul in Troas. Paul bid farewell to Aquila and Priscilla and all the brethren in Ephesus and left quickly for Troas with Gaius and Aristarchus (Acts 20:1-3) in order to meet up with Titus.

Paul arrived in Troas only to see that Titus was not there. He began to worry. He was so distressed by Titus' absence he could not preach to his brethren who were anxiously waiting to listen to him. He bid farewell and left for Macedonia in hope of finding him there (2Cor. 2:12-13). In Macedonia, there were so many problems to deal with Paul was besieged. «*For indeed, when we came to Macedonia, our bodies had no rest, but we were troubled on every side. Outside were conflicts, inside were fears*» (2 Cor. 7:5). Titus arrived and Paul breathed a deep sigh of relief. The news from Corinth was positive. The Corinthians had embraced Titus (2 Cor. 7:13) and had expressed zeal and were willing to rectify themselves. They mourned for the situation in their city (2Cor. 7:7). The factions had disappeared. Only the false apostles remained.

Paul was rejuvenated upon hearing the news. He wrote a fourth epistle to the Corinthians (the second epistle to the Corinthians) which Titus delivered personally to them (a third time). Paul wrote: «*Nevertheless God, who comforts the downcast, comforted us by the coming of Titus, and not only by his coming, but also by the consolation with which he was comforted in you, when he told us of your earnest desire, your mourning, your zeal for me, so that I rejoiced even more. For even if I made you sorry with my letter, I do not regret it; though I did regret it. For I perceive that the same epistle made you sorry, though only for a while. Now I rejoice… that your sorrow led to repentance. For you were made sorry in a Godly manner… For godly sorrow produces repentance leading to salvation not to be regretted…*» (2 Cor. 7:6-10).

In order to silence the false apostles (who were misleading the people) and strengthen the people, Paul had no choice but to display his virtues. He compared himself to them, stressing the suffering he experienced for the sake of preaching. He proved that he was more than a true Apostle of Christ:

«Seeing that many boast according to the flesh, I also will boast. For you have put up with fools gladly, since you yourselves are wise! For you put up with it if one brings you into bondage, if one devours you, if one takes from you, if one exalts himself, if one strikes you on the face… To our shame I say that we were too weak for that! But in whatever anyone is bold… I am bold also. Are they Hebrews? So am I. Are they Israelites? So am I. Are they the seed of Abraham? So am I. Are they ministers of Christ?… I am more: in labors more abundant, in stripes above measure, in prisons more frequently, in deaths often. From the Jews five times I receive forty stripes minus one. Three times I was beaten with rods; once I was stoned; three times I was shipwrecked; a night and a day I have been in the deep…» (2 Cor. 11:18-33)

4.1. «I SPEAK (...) FOOLISHLY...

It would be incorrect to assume that the humble Apostle was actually boasting about his experiences[2]. Paul was definitely not boasting. In fact he believed he was being foolish when he was writing the above verses of his epistle. *«When I speak, I speak not according to the Lord, but as it were, foolishly…»* (2 Cor. 11:17). Paul used this expression five times in verses 1 to 23 (Chapter 11). Most people tend to remind others again and again of the «good» things they have done (they usually do so not once, twice or three times, but constantly until the day they die), contrary to the Apostle Paul. What we consider to be virtuous Paul considers to be foolishness.

---

2 Paul believed that he was the *«least of all the apostles»* (1 Cor. 15:9). He also wrote that he was the «chief» sinner (1Tim.1:15). He was neither the least of all nor was he a sinner. He was a great Saint. One who approaches the Light uses it to see his infirmities and compares himself to Christ. Those who distance themselves from the light are in darkness and cannot see their weaknesses (and consider themselves saints).

5
Raising Money in Corinth

When Paul and Barnabas were in Antioch in 44 AD, «...*prophets came from Jerusalem to Antioch. Then one of them, named Agabus[3], stood up and showed by the Spirit that there was going to be a great famine throughout all the world, which also happened in the days of Claudius Caesar. Then the disciples, each according to his ability, determined to send relief to the brethren dwelling in Judea. This they also did, and sent it to the elders by the hands of Barnabas and Saul*» (Acts 11:27-30).

Paul, however, went even further. He asked the local Churches to raise money and send it to Jerusalem. He wrote to the Corinthians: «*On the first day of the week let each one of you lay something aside, storing up as he may prosper, that there be no collections when I come. And when I come, whomever you approve by your letters I will send to bear your gift to Jerusalem. But if it is fitting that I go also, they will go with me*» (1 Cor. 16:1-4).

At each stop he made on his way from Macedonia to Corinth, Paul reminded the local Churches not to forget the Church of Jerusalem, which was in need. The faithful responded to Paul's request and made contributions to help. «*For it pleased those from Macedonia and Achaia to make a certain contribution for the poor among the saints who are in Jerusalem. It pleased them indeed and they are their debtors*» (Rom. 15:26-27).

Paul arrived in Corinth in the winter. The residents of the city responded to his request and contributed money to the cause. Paul could have sent the money with one of his co-

---

[3] The prophets referred to in this verse were preachers who also received divine revelations from the Holy Spirit. They were ranked second to the Apostles (see 1 Cor. 12:27). The prophet Agabus travelled from Jerusalem to Caesarea (Palestine) to reveal to Paul the things he was going to experience in Jerusalem (Acts 21:10-12).

workers. Instead, he decided to deliver it personally because he wished to honor the local Church in Jerusalem and the people who contributed the money (it was not a matter of not trusting his co-workers). Paul wrote to the Romans from Corinth: «*Therefore when I have performed this deed* (the delivery of the money raised in Macedonia and Achaia to Jerusalem) *and have sealed to them this fruit, I shall go by way of you to Spain*» (Rom. 15:28).

Paul remained in Corinth for three months, waiting for winter to pass so that he could embark on his journey to Jerusalem (it was difficult for ships to sail during the winter months). During his stay in Corinth, he wrote his epistle to the Romans. Paul dictated, Tertius wrote the epistle (Rom. 16:22) and Phoebe, a servant of the Church, delivered it to Rome (Rom. 16:1). According to experts, the epistle to the Romans embodies all of Paul's teachings. It also influenced European civilization to a great extent.

5.1. AN ATTEMPT IS MADE ON HIS LIFE

The Jews of the city of Corinth were still at odds with Paul. The more they saw of him, the angrier they got. They decided to kill him at the port just before he embarked on his journey to Syria (he planned to go to Antioch first, then to Jerusalem). Paul was informed of the plot to kill him and there was a change of plan. He decided to travel to Philippi (on foot) with Luke and sail to Troas. He sent Timothy, Sopater, Aristarchus, Secundus, Gaius, Tychicus and Trophimus to the port in Corinth so as to confuse the Jews who planned to murder him (Acts 20:3-6).

6
Paul in Troas and Miletus

The trip from Samothrace to Troas was a difficult one due to inclement weather. The ship had to wait five days to enter the port. Paul and Luke finally met up with Timothy, Sopater, Aristarchus and the others. They stayed in Troas for seven days. Acts 20: 1-4).

On the last day before their departure, the Apostles and the local Christians gathered together in an upper room for the Divine Liturgy. Paul preached to the congregation, which did not want him to stop (nor did Paul want to stop, even though he was leaving in the morning).

The upper room was full of lamps, for it was night. A sudden noise interrupted the joyous atmosphere in the upper room. There were cries and screams. A young man named Eutychus had fallen asleep during Paul's sermon and fell out the window of the upper room (which was on the third story). Everyone had been concentrating so intensely on Paul's sermon; no one noticed that the young man had fallen asleep. The people ran downstairs but the young man was dead. Paul went down, embraced him and brought him back to life! However, Paul did not tell the people that the young man had died and that he brought him back to life. He said: «*Do not trouble yourselves, for his life is in him*» (Acts 20 :10). They went upstairs and Paul continued preaching until the morning. He bid them farewell and left for Assos (Acts 20:4-13).

6.1. PAUL BIDS FAREWELL TO THE ELDERS

Luke, Timothy and the others sailed to Assos, which was 32 km from Troas, opposite Lesbos. Paul chose to walk even though he had not slept at all. They met at the port and sailed to Miletus (which was just outside of Ephesus).

Paul wanted to visit Ephesus but he did not have time to because he wanted to be in Jerusalem for Pentecost. He called for the elders of Ephesus (who he had ordained himself) to go to Miletus and he spoke to them. Paul gave an emotional speech. It was the last time he would be seeing them:

And see now, I go bound in the spirit to Jerusalem, not knowing the things that will happen to me there, except that the Holy Spirit testifies in every city, saying that chains and tribulations await me. But none of these things move me; nor do I count my life dear to myself so that I may finish my race with joy, and the ministry which I received from the Lord Jesus… And indeed, now I know that you all, among whom I have gone preaching the kingdom of God, will see my face no more (Acts 20:22-25).

For I have not shunned to declare to you the whole counsel of God… Therefore watch and remember that for three years I did not cease to warn everyone night and day… Therefore I testify to you this day that I am innocent of the blood of all men… Therefore take heed to yourselves and to all the flock, among which the Holy Spirit has made you bishops[4], *to shepherd the church of God which He purchased with His own blood. For I know this, that after my departure savage wolves will come in among you, not sparing the flock. Also from among yourselves men will rise up speaking perverse things, to draw away the disciples after themselves. Therefore watch…* (Acts 20:26-31).

They kneeled and prayed. The elders cried knowing they would never see him again. They embraced him and kissed him. They accompanied Paul to the ship in tears. They would not let him leave for they could not bear the thought that they would never see him again.

7
The Journey to Jerusalem

Paul was well aware of the fact that he would face a passion of his own in Jerusalem. He knew he would find himself in the midst of three enemy factions: Christians who followed Mosaic Law, Felix the atrocious proconsul, and Jewish national-

---

4 The term «bishop» meant «overseer» in the world of idolatry. The same was true in the Old Testament. In other words, the term was not synonymous with a hierarchical position. Paul called high priests «overseers» so as to make the transition easy on idolaters. In his epistle to the Hebrews (which is directed at Jewish readers), he refers to bishops as high priests.

ists (who had multiplied much to the Romans' dismay[5]). The Apostle Paul was on their list of enemies. He would soon come face to face with them.

When Paul was in Corinth, he had a feeling that things were not going well in Jerusalem. He asked the Christians of Rome to pray on his behalf: «*Now I beg you, brethren, through the Lord Jesus Christ, and through the love of the Spirit, that you strive together with me in prayers to God for me, that I might be delivered from those in Judea...*» (Rom. 15:30-31).

On their way to Jerusalem Paul and the others stopped in Tyre for one week. They stayed with local Christians (Acts 21:3). «*They told Paul through the Spirit not to go up to Jerusalem*» (Acts 21:4). Paul was set on suffering for Christ. His life was meaningless unless he suffered for Christ.

Paul and the others sailed to Ptolemais where they stayed for one day and then walked to Caesarea (Palestine). The prophet Agabus arrived in Caesarea in search of Paul. He took Paul's belt, bound his hands and feet and said: «*Thus says the Holy Spirit[6], so shall the Jews at Jerusalem bind the man who owns this belt, and deliver him into the hands of the Gentiles*» (Acts 21:10-11). Luke wrote: «*Now when we heard these things, both we and those from that place pleaded with him not to go up to Jerusalem*» (Acts 21:12). They were in tears. Paul replied: «*What do you mean by weeping and breaking my heart? For I am ready not only to be bound, but also to die at Jerusalem for the name of the Lord Jesus*» (Acts 21:13). Luke further notes: «*So when he would not be persuaded, we ceased,*

---

5 Jewish nationalists carried swords (which resembled a sickle) under their garments. During major feast days, they would visit the temple, posing as pious pilgrims, kill pilgrims without anyone noticing them and escape. During the rule of Pontius Pilate, there was an uprising by Jewish nationalists against Romans in the temple area. Pilate sent the Roman army and the nationalists were slain (Luke 13:1-2). It is said that 20,000 Galileans were slain.

6 Why did the Holy Spirit not speak directly to Paul but to Agabus and the Christians at Tyre? It wanted to show the Christians in Tyre that Paul was going to suffer in Jerusalem and that he was determined to do so. The Holy Spirit did not warn Paul not to go to Jerusalem. It informed him of what was going to happen to him.

saying, "The will of the Lord be done". And after those days we packed and went up to Jerusalem» (Acts 21:14-15).

Large numbers of pilgrims made their way to Jerusalem for Pentecost. Christians from Caesarea also accompanied Paul on his trip to Jerusalem (Acts 21:16). The center of the festival was the Temple, where thousands of pilgrims gathered. Priests dressed in white would chop meat from the animals that were sacrificed and skillfully throw it onto the altar with accuracy. Nationalists would carry lambs on their shoulders for the sacrifice (meanwhile, they hid their swords under their garments which they would use to sacrifice humans…).

The time for Paul to go to the feast was approaching.

8
Jerusalem is in Uproar

The first thing Paul did when he arrived in Jerusalem was to meet James, the brother of the Lord and the elders of the local Church in order to give them the money that had been raised for the Church in Jerusalem. The elders of the city had gathered. The elderly James, with his white hair and beard, stood up front wearing a white sheet and no shoes (he never wore shoes). Paul stood by his side. The thousands of pilgrims who had gathered for the feast could be heard. The Christian pilgrims who followed Judaism had gathered and expressed their concern for the law and the fact that Paul was there.

Paul greeted the elders and submitted the money that had been raised as a token of love. He explained the details of his mission and stressed that many idolaters believed in the Lord (Acts 21:17-20). The elders said to him: «*You see brother, how many myriads of Jews there are who have believed, and they are all zealous for the law; but they have been informed about you that you teach all the Jews who are among the gentiles to forsake Moses, saying that they ought not to circumcise their children nor to walk according to the customs. What then? The assembly must certainly meet, for they will hear that you have come»* (Acts 21:20-22).

The elders suggested he go to the temple with four men who had taken a vow (who were with them) so he could take part in the purification with them. They told him to pay their expenses also. This would show the people that the accusations leveled against him were false (21:23-25).

Being humble, Paul decided to do what the elders told him. He went to the temple, and informed the priests concerning the vow the four men had made. They told him to offer fifteen lambs, fifteen baskets of bread, fifteen baskets of sweets, and fifteen flasks of wine (Num. 6:13-21). He paid for the expenses of the vow and he paid for their food for the week. Paul visited the temple every day for seven days. He took part in prayer which took place in the temple area together with the four men who had taken the vow (Acts 21:26-40).

The thousands of pilgrims who visited the city were confused by Paul's presence in the temple. The conservative Judeans were certain that he was trying to fool them. They planned to level serious accusations against him and turn the pilgrims against him. They planned to accuse him of defying Mosaic Law (Paul was trying to show that he respected the law).

On the last day of the vow (the seventh day), Paul was spotted in the temple. At the conclusion of morning prayer, Jews from Asia turned the crowd against him. They seized him and cried: «*Men of Israel, help! This is the man who teaches all men everywhere against the people, the law, and this place*» (Acts 21:28). News of the event spread around the city. A large crowd gathered at the temple seeking revenge against Paul. They dragged him out of the temple into the courtyard of the idolaters and shut the doors to prevent him from entering the temple and seeking asylum (Acts 21:30). They relentlessly beat him (they were determined to kill him) (Acts 21:32).

«*Now as they were seeking to kill him, news came to the commander* (Lysias) *of the garrison that all Jerusalem was in an uproar. He immediately took soldiers and centurions, and ran down to them. And when they saw the commander and the soldiers, they stopped beating Paul»* (Acts 21:31-32). The Roman commander (Lysias) was seeking an Egyptian rebel who misled 4,000 people to the Mount of Olives. He provided the people with swords but his rebellion was crushed. He fled into the wilderness and escaped. The commander was sure he had found the wanted rebel (Paul).

Paul was bound with two chains and led to the barracks which were next to the temple (Acts 21:33-34). When they reached the stairs which led from the temple to the barracks, they could not get by because of the crowd. *«Away with him!»* cried out the crowd (Acts 21:36).

«May I speak to you?» asked Paul. *«Can you speak Greek?»* asked Lysias. He was surprised when Paul spoke Greek because he thought he had apprehended the Egyptian rebel who was at large (Acts 21:37-38). Paul said: *«I am a Jew from Tarsus, in Cilicia, a citizen of no mean city; and I implore you, permit me to speak to the people»* (Acts 21:39). Paul stood on the stairs and motioned to the crowd to quieten down (Acts 21:40). Paul was an experienced speaker and he knew how to draw attention. He spoke to his fellow countrymen in Hebrew. When they heard him speak Hebrew, the crowd got even quieter (Acts 22:2).

Paul began by introducing himself: *«I am indeed a Jew, born in Tarsus of Cilicia, but brought up in this city at the feet of Gamaliel, taught according to the strictness of our fathers' law, and was zealous toward God as you all are today»* (Acts 22:3). He told them that he persecuted Christians and that on his way do Damascus, God Himself called him to be His Apostle. He explained that he respected the temple and the law and that they wrongly accused him of not doing so (Acts 22:3-20). The crowd listened to him carefully (Acts 22:22). When he told them that he received a command from God to preach to the Gentiles (Acts 22:21), they were outraged again. *«And they listened to him until this word, and then they* raised their voices and said, "Away with such a fellow from the earth, for he is not fit to live!"» (Acts 22:22) They tore off their clothes and threw them at him (Acts 22:23), which was considered worse than being spat on.

Lysias, who could not understand what was being said, ordered that Paul be questioned while scourged «*so that he might know why they shouted so against him*» (Acts 22:24). They took him to the barracks, took off his clothes and bound him to a pillar. Just as they were about to whip him, Paul said to the centurion: «*Is it lawful for you to scourge a man who is a Roman, and uncondemned?*» (Acts 22:25). The centurion went to Lysias and told him that Paul was a Roman citizen. Lysias asked him: «*Tell me, are you a Roman?*» Paul replied: «*Yes*» (Acts 22:27). They loosened him, gave him his clothes and placed him in a cell until they found out what had happened (Acts 22:29). Paul was still in chains.

9
Paul is Sent to Caesarea by Night

Lysias wanted to know why the Jews sought to kill Paul so he commanded that he be sent before the Sanhedrin (he commanded the chief priests and council to assemble) (Acts 22:30).

The Jews were well aware of the fact that only the chief priests and rulers of the people had the right to call the council together (Lysias had no right to do so) but it was to their benefit so they did not say a word to the Roman commander. They wanted to convict Paul and the Roman commander had facilitated their wish (Acts 22:30).

The council gathered in the room which was designated for council meetings (in the temple court). The infamous high priest Ananias was the head of the council. Paul was brought and set before the high priest. He said: «*Men and brethren, I have lived in all good conscience before God until this day*» (Acts 23:1).

Ananias could not tolerate hearing such words from an «apostate» and commanded that he be hit in the mouth (Ananias breached council procedure by not respecting Paul's right to speak). It was an indication that he did not consider Paul to be a Judean (which was the worst insult that could be spoken to a Jew). The other members of the council did not speak out against the high priest's violation of procedure, for they wished to convict Paul. Paul, however, did not remain silent. He said: «*God will strike you, you whitewashed wall…*» (Acts 23:3) (Paul's prophecy was fulfilled when Jewish nationalists slayed Ananias in his chamber). The other members of the council asked him: «*Do you revile God's priest?*» (Acts 23:4). Even though Paul was well aware that he was standing before the high priest (he could distinguish from his apparel) he said: «*I did not know, brethren, that he was the high priest*». The truth of the matter was he was not the high priest! Since Pentecost (after the Ascension of the Lord), the Apostles were bestowed authority to ordain priests, therefore, Ananias was no longer high priest for he did not believe in Christ (Acts 23:4-6) and was not a member of the Church.

Paul also cleverly took advantage of the dissension that existed between the Pharisees and the Sadducees. The Pharisees believed in the resurrection of the dead but the Sadducees did not (they mocked the Pharisees for believing so). Paul realized that his «trial» was not going to be a fair one and said: «*Men and brethren, I am a Pharisee, the son of a Pharisee; concerning the hope and the resurrection of the dead I am being judged!*» (Acts 23:6). Both groups fell into his trap. A commotion resulted. The Pharisees said: «*We find no evil in this man; but if a spirit or an angel has spoken to him, let us not fight against God*» (Acts 23:9). The Sadducees tried to seize him but the Pharisees protected Paul! Lysias commanded his soldiers to take him to the barracks for he feared they might kill him. Paul was distressed at the fact that he would not be able to fulfill his wish to go to Rome. Much to his surprise, the Lord appeared to Him at night and said: «*Be of good cheer,*

Paul; for as you have testified for Me in Jerusalem, so you must also bear witness at Rome» (Acts 23:11).

Jewish nationalists also sought to kill Paul. It is likely that they were informed by the Sadducees of the events that had taken place at the council. They decided to intervene. They swore not to eat or drink anything until they killed Paul. He was under heavy guard at the barracks which meant that they could not abduct him from the barracks. The nationalists went to the chief priest and elders and asked for their collaboration: «*We have bound ourselves under a great oath that we will eat nothing until we have killed Paul. Now you, therefore, together with the council, suggest to the commander that he be brought down to you tomorrow, as though you were going to make further inquiries concerning him; but we are ready to kill him before he comes near*» (Acts 23:14-15).

Someone «leaked» news of the plot to kill Paul. One of Paul's nephews (his sister's son) heard of the plot to kill Paul and he went to inform his uncle. Paul said to one of the centurions: «*Take this young man to the commander, for he has something to tell him*». Paul's nephew said to the commander: «*The Jews have agreed to ask that you bring Paul down to the council tomorrow, as though they were going to inquire more fully about him. But do not yield to them, for more than forty of them lie in wait for him, men who have bound themselves by an oath that they will neither eat nor drink till they have killed him…*» (Acts 23:17-22). The commander became concerned and told the young man not to tell anyone that he had revealed the plot to him (Acts 23:22).

The commander decided to send Paul to Felix, the governor of Judea, in Caesarea (which was approximately 100 km from Jerusalem): «*Prepare two hundred soldiers, seventy horsemen, and two hundred spearmen to go to Caesarea at the third hour of the night; and provide mounts to set Paul on, and bring him safely to Felix the governor*» (Acts 23:23-24). It must have been quite the sight seeing so many soldiers guarding an old, frail man!

In the morning, the chief priests and elders asked the commander to question Paul again. The nationalists were waiting by the roadside. They were boldly told that Paul had been sent to Felix, the governor of Judea in Caesarea. They went to Judea (no sleep for the wicked) together with the orator Tertullus (who played the part of their «attorney»). They were determined to win the «case» (Acts 24:1-2).

10

The «Warped» Governor

Felix lived at Herod's Praetorium (the king who killed the Forerunner). He had dealings with the Jewish nationalists (he arranged for the nationalists to murder the high priest Jonathan). He was somewhat of a tyrant and was driven by lust. He was married three times. His wife, Drusilla (the daughter of Herod Agrippas the first) was the wife of king Aziz of Hemese. When he first saw her, he went to Elymas and took her as his wife with the help of sorcery. This sinful individual was going to try the Apostle Paul! *«Deliver me, O my God, out of the hand of the wicked…»* wrote David (Ps. 71:4).

10.1. FELIX MEETS PAUL

Felix had some idea about the faith preached by Paul but he wanted to learn more. His wife (who was Jewish) also wished to learn more about Paul's «beliefs». They summoned Paul to the palace frequently in order to converse with him. Felix hoped to receive a bribe from him in order for him to release him (Acts 24:26), which is why he summoned him so often.

Paul knew about Felix's ways (he had been married three times and ruled like a tyrant) and talked to him about *«righteousness, self-control, and the judgment to come»* (Acts 24:25). He talked about self-control in reference to his lust and judgment with regard to the way he ruled.

The corrupt ruler was afraid (Acts 24:25) when he heard Paul's words, which is proof that everyone is concerned about Judgment Day (Christ is not a harsh, merciless judge, it is their sinful deeds and guilty conscience that cause them to view Christ in this manner). Felix, however, did not take his feelings any further. He did not repent and ask Paul for advice on what to do (as the prison guard in Philippi did [Acts 16:30]). Instead, he said to Paul: «*Go away for now; when I have a convenient time I will call for you*» (Acts 24:25). He never did call for him again.

Felix could see Paul's innocence, love and unselfish attitude after speaking to him on so many occasions. He had the authority to release him but he did nothing for he knew he would have to face the Jews (who crucified Christ twenty years earlier) and he did not want trouble from them. He chose not to release Paul even though he had been charged of misrule and Nero had threatened to remove him from office! Luke writes: «*...Felix, wanting to do the Jews a favor, left Paul bound*» (Acts 24:27).

Felix's successor, Porcius Festus also did as Felix had done[7].

11
Paul is Tried[8]

When Paul was handed over to Felix, the Roman soldiers gave the governor a letter from Lysias which wrote: «*Claudius Lysias, To the most excellent governor Felix: Greetings. This man*

---

[7] The first thing people of authority think about is their leadership (the exceptions are few and far between). Herod, who was seventy years old when Jesus was born, was afraid of losing his throne to the infant Jesus and killed all male infants two years of age and under (Matt. 2:16-18). «*Authority rids people of shame and turns them into beasts*» (St. John Chrysostom, Homily on Raising Children).

[8] Paul's trial in Caesarea was not a typical one. It was a trial that placed pressure on the authorities in Caesarea because Paul was a teacher of the law (he studied under Gamaliel) and a Roman citizen. He had the ability to cause «turmoil» and he did just that.

was seized by the Jews and was about to be killed by them. Coming with the troops I rescued him, having learned that he was a Roman. And when I wanted to know the reason they accused him, I brought him before their council. I found out that he was accused concerning questions of their law, but had nothing charged against him deserving of death or chains. And when it was told me that the Jews lay in wait for the man, I sent him immediately to you, and also commanded his accusers to state before you the charges against him. Farewell» (Acts 23:26-30). Felix said to Paul: «*I will hear you when your accusers also have come»* (Acts 23:35). Paul was then imprisoned in Herod's Praetorium.

Paul's accusers (the high priest Ananias, the chief priests and Tertullus) reached Caesarea after five days. The trial began. Tertullus spoke, saying: «*Seeing that through you (Felix) we enjoy great peace, and prosperity is being brought to this nation by your foresight, we accept it always and in all places, most noble Felix, with all thankfulness. Nevertheless, not to be tedious to you any further, I beg you to hear, by your courtesy, a few words from us»* (Acts 24:2-4). He described Paul as a man who did not respect the temple; therefore he was a threat to society because he was the leader of the heretical group the Nazarenes[9] which caused an uprising by Jews all over the world. Tertullus concluded: «*By examining him yourself you may ascertain all these things of which we accuse him»* (Acts 24:8). The Jews then joined in agreement with Tertullus' words.

It was Paul's turn to defend himself. Paul did not break out in a rage, nor did he uncover his accusers' secret plan to murder him. With respect to being accused of being the leader of a heresy, he stated: «*I worship the God of my fathers, believing all things which are written in the Law and in the Prophets»* (Acts 24:14). Paul proved that he was not opposed to Judaism. «*And they neither found me in the temple disputing with any-*

---

9 Christ's followers were called «Nazarenes» and «Galileans». The term «Christians» was first used in Antioch in reference to Christ's followers (Acts 11:26).

one nor inciting the crowd, either in the synagogues or in the city. Nor can they prove the things of which they now accuse me» (Acts 24:12-13). With respect to disrespecting the temple, he stated: «*Now after many years I came to bring alms and offerings to my nation, in the midst of which some Jews from Asia found me purified in the temple, neither with a mob nor with tumult. They ought to have been here before you to object if they had anything against me. Or else let those who are here themselves say if they have found any wrongdoing in me while I stood before the council*» (Acts 24:17-20).

Felix announced: «*When Lysias the commander comes down, I will make a decision on your case*» (Acts 24:22). Felix commanded the centurion to place Paul under guard, to give him freedom and to allow visitors to see him (Acts 24:23). Paul waited for the arrival of Lysias (who did not appear). Meanwhile, Felix submitted his resignation after having been asked to do so by the emperor.

Felix's successor, the commander of Syria, Porcius Festus, visited Jerusalem three days after being in office for matters concerning his rule. When the Jews heard about his visit, they took action and asked Festus to bring Paul to Jerusalem to be tried (meanwhile, the nationalists would be waiting by the roadside to kill Paul) (Acts 25:1-4). Festus, who was unaware of how much they despised Paul, wanted to exhibit his authority and told them that Paul would remain in Caesarea. He also said to them: «*Therefore, let those who have authority among you go down with me and accuse this man, to see if there is any fault in him*» (Acts 24:5).

Festus returned to Jerusalem and Paul was summoned to defend himself. When Festus saw how obsessed the Jews were with convicting Paul, he suggested Paul go to Jerusalem to be tried (Acts 25:9). Paul cleverly took advantage of the fact that he was a Roman citizen and appealed to Caesar (he asked to be tried in Rome!) (Act 25:11). The reason behind his decision was not his trust in the Roman judicial system but his deep desire to preach Christ in Rome (even under captivity). «*You have appealed to Caesar? To Caesar you shall go!*» replied Festus (Acts 25:11-12)

A reason, however, was required for someone to be sent to the emperor. Festus himself admitted that Paul was not guilty (Acts 25:25). He could not send Paul to the emperor without specifying what charges had been laid against him: «*For it seems to me unreasonable to send a prisoner and not to specify the charges against him*» (Acts 25:27). Paul was imprisoned once again (Acts 25:21) until Festus could think of something to write to the emperor concerning Paul so he could send him to Rome to be tried.

12
Paul's Case

In addition to Roman governors, the Jews were also subject to their own king, Agrippa the 2nd, king of Judea[10]. Agrippa's wife, Bernice, was his sister. The royal couple went to Caesarea to greet the new governor and wish him the best. Festus took the opportunity to mention Paul's case to Agrippa in the hopes of finding something to write concerning his case to the emperor (Acts 25:13-22). Festus told Agrippa that Paul's accusers «*had some questions against him about their own religion and about a certain Jesus, who had died, whom Paul affirmed to be alive*» (Acts 25:19). Agrippa replied: «*I also would like to hear the man myself*» (Acts 25:22). «*Tomorrow you shall hear him*», said Festus (Acts 25:22).

---

[10] Palstine was divided into four regions: Judea, Galilee, Samaria and Perea. Their respective capitals were Jerusalem, Capernaum, Sychar and Caesarea. In Jerusalem, there was an area near the Mount of Olives which was called Little Galilee. Galileans would gather there during their pilgrimages to Jerusalem for the celebration of feast days. When Christ told his disciples that He would go to Galilee after His Resurrection («*But after I have been raised, I will go before you to Galilee*». [Matt. 26:32]), He was referring to Little Galilee.

A hearing was held on the following day. The city's commanders and prominent men were present. «*Agrippa and Bernice had come with great pomp...*» (Acts 25:23). Paul was summoned to the auditorium. Festus opened the hearing by giving a brief account of what had happened. It was Paul's turn to defend himself.

Paul directed his words to the Judean king. He described his life and what had happened concerning his conversion. He concluded by saying: «*Therefore, having obtained help from God, to this day I stand, witnessing both to small and great, saying no other things than those which the prophets and Moses said would come-that the Christ would suffer, that He would be the first to rise from the dead, and would proclaim light to the Jewish people and to the Gentiles*» (Acts 26:22-23).

When Festus heard his words, he boldly interrupted Paul saying: «*Paul, you are beside yourself! Much learning is driving you mad!*»[11] (Acts 26:24) Paul replied: «*I am not mad, most noble Festus, but speak the words of truth and reason*». Paul then took advantage of Agrippa's presence and said: «*For the king, before whom I also speak freely, knows these things; for I am convinced that none of these things escapes his attention, since this thing was not done in a corner. King Agrippa, do you believe the prophets? I know that you do believe*» (Acts 26:24-27). The king replied: «*You almost persuade me to become a Christian*». Paul said: «*I would to God that not only you, but also all who hear me today, might become both almost and altogether such as I am, except for these chains*»[12].

---

11 What bothered Festus? It was the word of God, which is alive, dynamic and a «two-edged sword» that pierces «*the division of soul and sprit, and of joints and marrow, and is a discerner of the thoughts and intents of the heart*». (Heb. 4:12). So, when Festus (who lived a lie) heard the truth (the word of God), he was upset and called Paul «mad» in order to satisfy his conscience.

12 One gets the impression that Paul was complaining about being bound. This was not so. Paul was glad to suffer for Christ (2Cor. 11:30). However, this is how Paul felt. The unfaithful did not share his sentiments. When Paul spoke to king Agrippa and the entire hearing, he «stooped» to their level. He spoke to them in accordance to their spiritual and psychological state. «*The saints try to persuade their adversaries to believe in*

When Paul had finished his defense, the king, Bernice, Festus and everyone in the auditorium left and concluded: «*This man is doing nothing deserving of death or chains*» (Acts 26:32). Agrippas said to Festus: «*This man might have been set free if he had not appealed to Caesar*» (Acts 26:32).

In his letter to the emperor, Festus referred to Paul's case as being a religious one concerning a Jew. Paul was sent to Rome along with other prisoners. Julius, a centurion of the Augustan Regiment (Acts 27:1) was in charge of seeing that the prisoners reached Rome. He took a liking to Paul and treated him kindly (Acts 27:3:43).

12.1. BOARDING THE SHIP

It is estimated that Paul set sail for Rome in the middle of August, 61 AD. He was at sea for three months (August to October). Paul travelled with a group of convicts who were being sent to Rome to be fed to the lions in the coliseum. Paul, on the other hand, was being sent to Rome to be questioned by Caesar.

There were no comforts on the ship he was sailing on, as was the case with Paul's entire apostolic mission. Paul had to sleep in shackles on the deck of the ship and was under close guard. Luke, who described the epic journey in writing (Acts 27:2-44, 28:1-15), accompanied him.

13
The Journey to Rome

At the time of the Apostles, sailing was much more dangerous than it is today. The ships used were much more fragile than today's vessels. They were in danger of splitting open in two when sailing in rough seas, which is why they avoided

Christ. They do not try to escape from them». (St. John Chrysostom, *Concerning the Statues*, 16:4)

sailing in winter. The wind determined how fast they could travel and the sun and stars indicated direction. When it was overcast, sailors were unsure of where they were heading. This is why the Church prays for those who are sailing (in the Divine Liturgy).

The journey to Rome was full of danger (Acts 27:1-14). The ship was in a «struggle» against nature in its voyage to Rome. Paul, though, was not concerned because the Lord told him that he would go to Rome (Acts 23:11). He knew that even if the ship sank, he would make it to Rome alive. The ship did in fact sink and Paul made it to Rome alive!

After setting sail from Caesarea, the ship stopped in Myra of Asia Minor. The prisoners (including Paul) boarded a large ship carrying wheat which had set sail from Alexandria and was on its way to Puteoli in Italy (Acts 27:4-6). There were a total of 276 passengers on board (Acts 27:37). The ship set sail and trouble was just around the corner. Strong winds kept the ship off course. The ship was in Crete but it should have already reached Rome had the weather not been inclement. Winter had just begun when the ship was at Fair Havens on the southern coast of Crete (Acts 27:7-8). The trip had to be postponed. The captain, the centurion and everyone else held an emergency meeting. Paul was also present. He said: «*Men, I perceive that this voyage will end with disaster and much loss, not only of the cargo and ship, but also our lives*». (Acts 27:10) They did not listen to Paul and they set sail for Phoenix (Crete). Soon after they had set off, a tempestuous wind (typhoon) arose (Acts 27:9-13). It was overcast for fourteen days and the huge waves relentlessly struck the vessel making it impossible to navigate the ship.

The ship's hull was in danger of splitting open. The sailors did all they could to save the ship. They tied the ship together with ropes and they threw much of the cargo into the sea to make the ship lighter but they were still in danger. They had no choice but to throw all of the ship's equipment overboard (Acts 27:19). They were unsure of where they were and where they were heading. Luke wrote: «*Now when neither sun nor stars appeared for many days, and no small tempest beat on us, all hope that we would be saved was finally given up*» (Acts 27:20).

Paul then rose and said: «*Men, you should have listened to me, and not have sailed from Crete and incurred this disaster and loss. And now I urge you to take heart, for there will be no loss of life among you, but only of the ship*» (Acts 27:21-22). «*For there stood by me this night an angel of the God to whom I belong and whom I serve, saying, "Do not be afraid, Paul; you must be brought before Caesar; and indeed God has granted you all those who sail with you". Therefore take heart men, for I believe God that it will be just as it was told me. However, we must run aground on a certain island*» (Acts 27:21-26)[13].

The ship was approaching land. «*And the sailors were seeking to escape from the ship, when they had let down the skiff into the sea, under pretense of putting out anchors from the prow*». Paul said to the centurion and the soldiers: «*Unless these men stay in the ship, you cannot be saved*» (Acts 27:30-31). The soldiers cut the ropes and let the skiff fall into the sea.

As they waited for dawn to arrive Paul urged them to eat something: «*Today is the fourteenth day you have waited and continued without food, and eaten nothing. Therefore I urge you to take nourishment, for this is for you survival, since not a hair will fall from the head of any of you*» (Acts 27:33-34). Paul took bread in his hands, prayed and ate. When they saw him do so, they ate also. «*When they had eaten enough, they lightened the ship and threw out the wheat into the sea*» (Acts 27:38).

Dawn finally arrived. They were not certain where they were but they were relieved to see land. Some must have mocked Paul for saying the ship would be lost. The ship had

---

13 Why did God not appear to Paul on the fist day of the storm? God chooses to instruct us in the manner He chooses fit. Being aware of the fact that temptations often benefit us, he «exposes» us to them. In Philippi, God «forcefully» intervened after Paul had been imprisoned (Acts 16:25-40). When he was distressed while in Caesarea, God appeared to him and told him that he would travel to Rome (Acts 23:11). God judged that now was the right time to encourage Paul and He did.

run aground into a sandy shore, however, the stern of the ship was being relentlessly hit by waves and was coming apart (Acts 27:39-41). A port lay ahead. When the prisoners saw land up ahead, they prepared to escape. When the soldiers realized what was about to happen, they quickly decided to execute the prisoners, including Paul. Julius, the centurion, stopped them for he wanted to save Paul (Acts 27:43). The centurion commanded the prisoners who knew how to swim to jump into the sea. The rest used parts of the ship to make it ashore (Acts 27:43-44).

13.1. IN MALTA

When the castaways set foot ashore, they were told they were in Malta. News of their arrival spread around the island. The natives ran to the shore to help the castaways. They gathered wood and lit a fire to warm the castaways who were exposed to the rain and cold. Paul also went to work. He collected sticks to throw into the fire[14] (Acts 28:1-4).

The magistrate of the island, Publius, allowed the castaways to stay on his estate until they could find somewhere to stay for the winter. Paul healed his sick father and when the news spread, many sick people were brought to Paul and he healed them also. They stayed on the island for three months (from the beginning of November in 61 AD to the beginning of February in 62 AD). The residents of the island received the castaways with courtesy. When they left the island (on February 10th) the residents provided them with the necessities they needed for the trip (Acts 28:7-10).

The Maltese people named the coast where the shipwreck took place *The Coast of the Apostle Paul* in memory of the event, which is celebrated annually on the 10th of February.

---

[14] The inhabitants of Malta were migrants from Carthage in North Africa. They spoke a Phoenician dialect that was similar to Aramaic. Paul was able to communicate with them and played the part of interpreter.

14
In Rome

It was common for ships to anchor in the closest ports they could dock in when travelling during the winter. In the winter of 61-62 AD, a large ship loaded with wheat which had embarked from Egypt was in Malta waiting for the winter to pass. The ship's final destination was Puteoli.

When the weather cleared up, the castaways boarded the ship and set sail. The first stop was Syracuse, the capital of Sicily. They stayed there for three days. Julius allowed Paul to leave the ship. Paul took advantage of the opportunity to preach to the residents of Syracuse.

Their next stop was Rhegium (which was on the channel which separates Sicily from Italy), where they were forced to stop due to inclement weather. The weather quickly improved and they set sail for Puteoli. They reached the port in two days[15] (Acts 28:11-15).

It was the first ship that reached the city after the harsh winter that had passed. There was an uprising every time a ship arrived from Egypt. The residents ran to the harbor cheering (in this specific case, they were happier than usual because they had been waiting for so long). The grunts and roars of the tigers and lions on the ship were a disheartening reminder for the prisoners on board of what lay ahead for them. A seven day journey to Rome on foot awaited them.

14.1. A WARM WELCOME FOR PAUL

In his epistle to the Romans (which he wrote three years earlier), Paul told them that he would visit them. They had also heard many things concerning Paul and were anxious to meet him. The Christians in Puteoli had informed those in Rome

---

15 The port of Puteoli was the final destination of ships carrying wheat from Africa. The ships also carried tigers and lions for the coliseums in Puteoli and Rome.

of his arrival. They took to the streets in anticipation of his arrival. This first group of Christians to welcome him walked a distance of 60 km from Rome in order to do so (a fifteen hour walk)! Julius the centurion and the prisoners were witnesses to the extraordinary meeting that took place between the Christians of Rome and Paul. They took the Via Appia which was considered the finest in the world, and proceeded with great joy to Rome. A second group of Christians arrived to meet Paul at a distance of approximately 48 km outside of the city. The second meeting was more formal as the group most likely consisted of representatives of the local Church (Priscilla and Aquila must have also been present). «*When Paul saw them, he thanked God and took courage*» (Acts 28:15). This is an indication that Paul was discouraged before seeing them.

Paul entered Rome in chains, accompanied by brigades of Christians. He entered as a Messiah, not as a criminal.

14.2. **UNDER ARREST**

The headquarters of the Imperial Guard was housed in a large building that was as large as a city block. The skilled and honorable General Burros was the captain of the guard (he and Seneca were Nero's instructors). Julius handed Paul over to him upon arriving at the headquarters. When Burros read Paul's file, he developed a favorable opinion of Paul. He ordered the guards to treat him well and he placed him in a cell on his own (the other prisoners were placed together in large cells). Luke writes: «*Now when we came to Rome, the centurion delivered the prisoners to the captain of the guard; but Paul was permitted to dwell by himself with the soldier who guarded him*» (Acts 28:16).

Paul may have been alone but he was not free. He was bound to a chain and was guarded night and day (Acts 28:11). The soldier who guarded him was constantly present in his cell, even when Paul had visitors. A different soldier guarded him every day, which meant that Paul had to face a different person (whith different traits) each day.

Paul's case-*the religious case of a Jew*-was insignificant to the imperial court. This explained why Paul's trial was delayed. There are no records of how long Paul had to wait to be tried but if we take into account the fact that his spiritual children visited him from far away and that he wrote four epistles (the epistles to the Ephesians, Philippians, Philemon and Colossians), it is safe to assume that he waited for approximately a year (or more) to be tried.

14.3. AN UNEXPECTED VISIT

News of Paul's confinement in Rome spread to all of the Churches in Asia Minor, Macedonia, etc. In Philippi, an uprising took place when Christians were informed of what had happened to Paul. They decided to help their spiritual father any way they could (by sending money, food and clothing). Epaphroditus was willing to travel to Rome. Epaphroditus arrived in Rome but Paul could not rejoice in his arrival because as soon as he arrived, Epaphroditus became ill to the point of death. The Philippians heard the news. Epaphroditus was concerned about the Philippians because he was aware of the fact that they were worried about his health. His health eventually improved and he made a complete recovery. Paul sent the Philippians an epistle in which he wrote: «*Yet I considered it necessary to send to you Epaphroditus, my brother, fellow worker, and fellow soldier, but your messenger and the one who ministered to my need; since he was longing for you all, and was distressed because you had heard that he was sick. For indeed he was sick almost unto death; but God had mercy on him, and not only on him but on me also, lest I should have sorrow upon sorrow. Therefore, I sent him the more eagerly, that when you see him again you may rejoice, and I may be less sorrowful. Receive him therefore in the Lord with all gladness, and hold such men in esteem; because for the work of Christ he came close to death, not regarding his life, to supply what was lacking in your service toward me*» (Phil. 2:25-30).

14.4. PAUL GRIEVES OVER BARNABAS

One day, Paul received an unexpected visit. John Mark, Barnabas' nephew had come to visit him (Col. 4:10). Mark buried his uncle in Cyprus (Paul's friend from childhood) and went to Rome to see Paul.

The news of Barnabas' death crushed Paul. He mourned and wept but did not despair because he believed the following: «*But I do not want you to be ignorant, brethren, concerning those who have fallen asleep, lest you sorrow as others who have no hope. For if we believe that Jesus died and rose again, even so God will bring with Him those who sleep in Jesus*» (1 Thess. 4:13-14). «*For since by man came death, by Man also came the resurrection of the dead. For as in Adam all die, even so in Christ all shall be made alive. But each one in his own order: Christ the firstfruits, afterward those who are Christ's at His coming*». (1 Cor. 15:21-23).

15
The Sermon in Chains

Paul greatly desired to preach in Rome (Rom. 15:24,28). However, Paul had come to Rome as a criminal, not as a preacher. He was certain, however, that the Lord would deliver him from his conviction, for wrote: «*And we know that all things work together for good to those who love God…*» (Rom. 8:28). His conviction truly had a positive outcome.

From the moment he appealed to Caesar (Acts 25:11), he was under imperial protection. No one could lay a hand on him. Paul may have been in chains and under guard but he was able to do what he desired to do, preach. His hands may have been bound but his mouth was not. Paul wrote that «*the word of God is not chained*» (2 Tim. 2:8). «*But I want you to know, brethren, that the things which happened to me have actually turned out for the furtherance of the gospel…*» (Phil. 1:12).

15.1. THE JEWS

Rome had a population of approximately 30,000 Jews. Normally, they would have made life difficult for Paul but they could not because Paul was under imperial protection. Paul could not go to the synagogue to preach so he called the Jewish leaders to visit him (Acts 28:17) in order to explain the reason for his arrest (he was certain they knew what he was accused of). He explained that he was not an adversary of their people and customs. He did not mention a word with respect to the harsh treatment he was subjected to by his fellow countrymen in Jerusalem (he did not mention that he was arrested without being told why and that he was beaten in the temple). Paul's purpose was to rid people of their passions and evil. He did not wish to further develop them. He said: «*Men and brethren, though I have done nothing against our people or the customs of our fathers, yet I was delivered as a prisoner from Jerusalem into the hands of the Romans, who, when they had examined me, wanted to let me go, because there was no cause for putting me to death. But when the Jews spoke against it, I was compelled to appeal to Caesar, not that I had anything of which to accuse my nation. For this reason I have called for you, to see you and speak with you, because for the hope of Israel I am bound with this chain*» (Acts 28:17-20). They replied: «*We neither received letters from Judea concerning you, nor have any of the brethren who came reported or spoken any evil of you. But we desire to hear from you what you think; for concerning this sect, we know that it is spoken against everywhere*» (Acts 28:21).

They arranged to have a discussion with him and returned to their homes. News of the upcoming religious discussion was heard throughout the greater area.

The day of discussion finally arrived. The Jews gathered where Paul was staying, eager to hear what this strange man had to say. It was the last time Paul would speak to an all-Jewish audience. He spoke from morning to evening about the Kingdom of God and the prophets, trying to persuade them that Christ was the Messiah, but to no avail. He concluded his sermon by referring to the book of Isaiah: «*The Holy Spirit spoke rightly through Isaiah the prophet saying, "Go to this people and say: Hearing you will hear, and shall not understand; and seeing you will see, and not perceive; for the hearts of this people have grown dull. Their ears are hard of hearing, and their eyes they have closed, lest they should see with their eyes and hear with their ears, lest they should understand with their hearts and turn, so that I should heal them". "Therefore let it be known to you that the salvation of God has been sent to the Gentiles, and they will hear it!"*» (Acts 28:25-28).

The Jews left and a great dispute broke out. Others believed while others refused to.

16
The Epistles Written While in Custody

Paul cared for his spiritual children as a mother cares for her children. He «bore» his spiritual children with great difficulty. He did all he could for his spiritual children while he was under confinement. He prayed for them night and day (Eph. 1:15-19, Col. 1:3,9, Phil. 1:2-5) and wrote epistles to them.

The epistles to the Ephesians, Philippians, Colossians and to Philemon were written in the years 61-63 AD while Paul was under confinement.

16.1. THE EPISTLE TO THE EPHESIANS

Paul's disciple Tychicus, who was from Ephesus, visited Paul in Rome. Paul summoned him to his cell and gave him the epistle he had written to the Ephesians so that he could deliver it personally. He wrote:

«*Tychicus, a beloved brother and faithful minister in the Lord, will make all things known to you, whom I have sent to you for this very purpose, that you may know our affairs, and that he may comfort your hearts*» (Eph. 6:21-23).

But fornication and all uncleanness or covetousness, let it not even be named among you, as is fitting for saints; neither filthiness nor foolish talking, nor coarse jesting, which are not fitting, but rather giving of thanks, for this you know, that no fornicator, unclean person, nor covetous man, who is an idolater, has any inheritance in the kingdom of Christ and God (Eph. 5:3-6).

See then that you walk circumspectly, not as fools but as wise, redeeming the time, because the days are evil. Do not be unwise, but understand what the will of the Lord is (Eph. 5:15-17).

16.2. THE EPISTLE TO PHILEMON

Philemon was a wealthy man from Colosse (near Ephesus) and a member of the Church. Paul was his spiritual father. Philemon's servant left Colosse after stealing money from his master and fled to Rome (which was a haven for fugitives). He heard that Paul was in Rome and he visited him. He filled Paul in on his life. Paul showed Philemon's ex-servant love and kindness and he became a Christian. Paul called him Onesimus, which means «useful», in contrast to his previous lifestyle.

Onesimus was truly useful. Paul considered keeping him with him so that Onesimus could help him with his needs, however, by law, Onesimus was still subject to Philemon and Paul did not want to keep him without his master's consent (Philem. 8-14). He decided to send Onesimus back to Philemon and he sent him an epistle in which he asked Philemon to accept Onesimus as if he were Paul (his spiritual father): *«Therefore, though I might be very bold in Christ to command you what is fitting, yet for love's sake I rather appeal to you-being such a one as Paul, the aged, and now also a prisoner of Jesus Christ-I appeal to you for my son Onesimus, whom I have begotten while in my chains, who was once unprofitable to you, but now is profitable to you and to me. I am sending him back. You therefore receive him, that is, my own heart, whom I wished to keep with me, that on your behalf he might minister to me in my chains for the gospel. But without your consent I wanted to do nothing... If then you count me as a partner, receive him as you would me. But if he has wronged you or owes anything, put that on my account... Yes, brother, let me have joy from you in the Lord; refresh my heart in the Lord»* (Philem. 8-20).

16.3. THE EPISTLE TO THE PHILIPPIANS

Epaphroditus delivered Paul's epistle to the Philippians after visiting Paul in Rome. It is truly a gem.

16.3.1. LIFE AND DEATH

For... with all boldness, as always, so now also Christ will be magnified in my body, whether by life or by death. For to me, to live is Christ, and to die is gain... For I am hard-pressed between the two, having a desire to depart and be with Christ, which is far better. Nevertheless to remain in the flesh is more needful for you. And being confident of this, I know that I shall remain and continue with you all for our progress and joy of faith... (Phil. 1:20-26).

16.3.2. ADVICE

Only let your conduct be worthy of the gospel of Christ, so that whether I come and see you or am absent, I may hear of your affairs, that you stand fast in one spirit, with one mind striving together for the faith of the gospel... (Phil. 1:27-28).

«*Fulfill my joy by being like-minded, having the same love, being of one accord, of one mind. Let nothing be done through selfish ambition or conceit, but in lowliness of mind let each esteem others better than himself. Let each of you look out not only for his own interests, but also for the interests of others.* (Phil. 2:2-5). *Therefore my beloved, as you have always obeyed, not as in my presence only, but now much more in my absence, work out your own salvation with fear and trembling; for it is God who works in you both to will and to do for His good pleasure*» (Phil. 2:12-13).

«*Do all things without complaining and disputing, that you may become blameless and harmless, children of God without fault in the midst of a crooked and perverse generation, among whom you shine as lights in the world, holding fast the word of life, so that I may rejoice in the day of Christ that I have not run in vain or labored in vain»* (Phil. 2:14-16).

16.4. THE EPISTLE TO THE COLOSSIANS

Fanatic Jews could not bear to see Christianity spread. Seeing that they could not attempt to persuade Christians to change their faith, they decided to collaborate with the Gentiles and they mixed the Gospel with foreign teachings from other religions, philosophy and Judean customs. Because of the fact that Ephesus was like an «impenetrable» fortress, they put their plan into action in Colosse. The Christians in Colosse were confused when they heard these teachings from Judeans and Gentiles alike. Paul's disciple Epaphras, the bishop of Colosse, quickly went to Rome to ask for Paul's advice on the matter. Paul sent the Colossians an epistle in which he wrote:

Beware lest anyone cheat you through philosophy and empty deceit, according to the tradition of men, according to the basic principles of the world, and not according to Christ. For in Him dwells all the fullness of the Godhead bodily; and you are complete in Him, who is the head of all principality and power (Col. 2:8-10).

Therefore, if you died with Christ from the basic principles of the world, why, as though living in the world, do you subject yourselves to regulations-Do not touch, do not taste, do not handle, which all concern things which perish with the using-according to the commandments and doctrines of men? (Col. 2:20-23).

16.4.1. SOLID FOUNDATIONS: SPIRITUAL STRUGGLE

Paul then encourages the Christians in Colosse to fight a spiritual battle in order to strengthen them in Christ. He tells them to remain clean in body (to abstain from sins of the flesh) and in spirit (to avoid enmity, evil thoughts). He warns them that if they do not do so, their relationship with Christ will be based on a weak foundation and will be in danger of collapsing.

16.4.2. A CLEAN BODY

If then you were raised with Christ, seek those things which are above, where Christ is, sitting at the right hand of God. Set your mind on things above, not on things of the earth. For you died and your life is hidden with Christ in God... Therefore put to death your members which are on the earth: fornication, uncleanness, passion, evil desire, and covetousness, which is idolatry. Because of these things the wrath of God is coming upon the sons of disobedience in which you yourselves once walked when you lived in them (Col. 3:1-7).

16.4.3. A CLEAN SOUL

Therefore, as the elect of God, holy and beloved, put on tender mercies, kindness, humility, meekness, long-suffering; bearing with one another, and forgiving one another, if anyone has a complaint against another; even as Christ forgave you, so you also must do. But above all these things put on love, which is the bond of perfection. And let the peace of God rule in your hearts, to which also you were called in one body... (Col. 3:12-15).

17
Paul is Acquitted: A New Beginning

Things were about to become gloomy in Rome. Nero, the Roman Emperor from 54-68 AD, was soon to begin his harsh persecution of Christianity. He even killed his own mother! His teachers Seneca and Borrus eventually abandoned him and went into hiding because they feared for their lives (they should have gone into hiding out of shame for their student).

Nero appointed Tigelinus (his «partner in crime») and Rufus captains of the imperial guard. Because of the fact that Tigelinus was caught up in Nero's plans, Paul's life now lay in the hands of Rufus. There were two possible verdicts: death or acquittal. Rufus carefully examined Paul's file and determined that he was innocent. He signed his release and Paul was acquitted (this decision meant that Christianity was permitted in Rome). It was the summer of 63 AD. At the time Paul was released, James the brother of the Lord was killed in Jerusalem.

Paul was finally released from the chains he was bound in (which he wore since he was held captive in Caesarea!). He was a free man. He was free to preach by law, therefore, the Jews could not persecute him (he was under the protection of the emperor's verdict). «*Then Paul dwelt two whole years in his own rented house, and received all who came to him, preaching the kingdom of God and teaching the things which concern the Lord Jesus Christ with all confidence, no one forbidding him*» (Acts 28:30-31).

17.1. PAUL CONTINUES PREACHING!

Even though Paul was old and had gone through many trials and tribulations, he still had the strength to continue preaching. He continued to strengthen the Churches he had established with great pain and effort. The mere thought of Christ on the Cross did not allow Paul to rest. His body may have been old and frail but his heart was strong.

Initially, he had planned to go to Spain (Rom. 15:24) but he went to Crete instead (perhaps he realized that the Cretans were in need when he stayed in Fair Havens on his way to Rome).

The island of Crete was a «bridge» that linked Greece and Alexandria, the city with the largest harbor in Asia and Africa. The Cretans, as a result, had been influenced greatly by wealth, trade and communication. Paul agreed with Epimenidis' comment: «*Cretans are always liars, evil beasts, lazy gluttons*» (Titus 2:12-13).

However, Crete was not a stranger to Christianity because Cretans were in Jerusalem on the day of Pentecost (Acts 2:11) and they informed their countrymen concerning what happened in Jerusalem when they returned home. Although there were no local Churches in Crete (ministers and overseers), there were Christians who believed in Christ.

Paul travelled to Crete with Titus and they began preaching with the purpose of establishing local Churches. He appointed Titus overseer of Crete so that he would preach and ordain ministers in each city (Titus 1:5). Paul continued his journey.

17.2. PAUL IN SPAIN

Clement, the bishop of Rome (1st century AD) kept the Christians in Corinth up to date concerning Paul's whereabouts (1 Cor. 5:6). He wrote that Paul traveled from Crete to the far west (which referred to Spain at the time). There are local traditions in Spain that verify this. For example, in the city of Tortoza, tradition holds that Paul ordained a bishop named Rufus. The same tradition exists in the city of Estilla.

18
Paul Bids Farewell to the Churches

Although Paul had grown old and was extremely wary from the difficulties he had faced in his turbulent lifetime, he wished to bid farewell to the Churches he had established. And so he began his final farewell journey!

Paul departed from Spain and travelled to Crete, where he met up with Titus. He preached and strengthened the new Church in Crete, bid farewell to Titus and all of his spiritual children and left. Each and every departure was disheartening for Paul. He proceeded to Corinth with Timothy, Erastus and Trophimus. He preached, carried out the Divine Liturgy and strengthened his brethren. He left Erastus behind (as a «gift») (2 Tim. 4:20), bid farewell and sailed to Asia Minor.

His first stop was Miletus. He strengthened the brethren. He left Trophimus in Miletus (who had fallen ill) (2 Tim. 4:20), bid farewell and departed for Ephesus. At every stop, he preached, carried out the Divine Liturgy, bid the people farewell and departed. He left his beloved and chosen co-worker Timothy in Ephesus. He felt as if one of his limbs had been severed. Nevertheless, he did it for the benefit of the Church. The feeling was mutual for Timothy, who was in tears for he was bidding farewell to his spiritual father forever (2 Tim. 1:4). Paul left for Troas which was his final stop in Asia Minor. He stayed with Carpus, to whom he left all of his belongings (his cloak, books and parchments) (2 Tim. 4:13).

18.1. THE EPISTLE TO TITUS

When Paul was in Asia Minor for the last time, he sent Titus (who was overseer of the new Church in Crete) an epistle. He began by writing: «*To Titus, a true son in our common faith...*»

But as for you, speak... that the older men be sober, reverent, temperate, sound in faith, in love, in patience; the older women likewise, that they be reverent in behavior, not slanderers, not given to much wine, teachers of good things-that they admonish the young women to love their husbands, to love their children... that the word of God may not be blasphemed. Likewise, exhort the young men to be sober-minded, in all things showing yourself to be a pattern of good works... that cannot be condemned...(Titus 2;2-8).

Paul travelled to Macedonia. He bid farewell to Philippi (which offered Paul a large degree of support while he was imprisoned), Thessalonica and Berea.

18.2. THE FIRST EPISTLE TO TIMOTHY

It was impossible for Paul to forget his beloved son Timothy in Ephesus. He wished to advise him and strengthen him and thus felt the need to write to him. Paul sent Timothy a personal epistle from Macedonia. He wrote: «*As I urged you when I went into Macedonia-remain in Ephesus that you may charge some that they teach no other doctrine, nor give heed to the fables and endless genealogies, which cause disputes rather than godly edification which is in faith»* (1 Tim. 1:2-4).

Do not rebuke an older man, but exhort him as a father, younger men as brothers, older women as mothers, younger women as sisters, with all purity (1 Tim. 5:1-3).

«Command those who are rich in the present age not to be haughty, nor to trust in uncertain riches but in the living God, who gives us richly all things to enjoy. Let them do good, that they be rich in good works, ready to give, willing to share, storing up for themselves a good foundation for the time to come, that they may lay hold on eternal life» (1 Tim. 6:17-20).

18.3. NICOPOLIS

Nicopolis was the largest city in Epirus[16]. Paul had never visited the city before but this time he was determined to do so. He wrote to Titus: *«When I send Artemas to you, or Tychicus, be diligent to come to me at Nicopolis, for I have decided to spend the winter there»* (Titus 3:12).

Paul preached and established the Church of Nicopolis, where he spent his last winter with Titus. When winter had come to an end, Titus went to Dalmatia (2 Tim. 4:10) to preach and Paul went to Rome (to become a martyr for Christ). Paul's trip to Rome was to be his final journey.

---

[16] Nicopolis is derived from the Greek words for victory (nike) and city (polis). It was given its name by Caesar Augustus in honor of his defeat of Anthony in the battle of Actium in 31 BC.

19
Paul's Last Moments

Lust can be compared to fire. When a fire gets out of control, it burns everything in its way and increases in intensity. The same is true of sensuality. When lustful thoughts emerge, they «demand» to be fulfilled. The more they are fulfilled, the more harm is done.

This was the case with the Roman Emperor Nero. He had the best clown at his disposal, Alityrus, who provided him with laughter and entertainment. His mistress Sabina provided him with bodily pleasure. Even so, Nero felt empty inside. He was searching for something unique to break the monotony he was feeling. He considered burning down the city (the great monument of civilization)! He was not the least bit concerned about the residents and their homes. The only thing that mattered to him was seeking pleasure.

On the night of the 19th of June, 64 AD, Nero commanded his servants to set the city on fire! The fire raged for seven days. Three of Rome's fourteen districts were completely burned down and seven were severely damaged. Only three remained unharmed. Nero took great pleasure in the sight.

An insurrection by the people who lost their homes and property resulted. Nero blamed the Jews for the fire while the Jews put the blame on the Christians. Nero's mistress (who worshipped the Jewish faith) and Alityrus his clown (who happened to be Jewish) persuaded Nero to put the blame on the Christians.

Thus began the relentless persecution against the «guilty» Christians. Guards broke into Christian homes and arrested them. Some were executed, others were crucified and others were thrown to the lions. Christians were also hung upside-down on pillars or burned to death at places where Romans gathered at night for entertainment (their burning bodies were used as a source of light!)

Christianity had suddenly become a threat to Rome overnight.

19.1. PAUL ARRIVES IN ROME

Paul, being the Christian leader, was number one on the most wanted list. By coincidence, the fire in Rome broke out shortly after Paul left for his final journey to the Churches. Paul was accused of planning the fire and leaving. In the spring of 67 AD, Paul returned to Rome. The fire which burned down the city may have been put out; however, the «fire» in the hearts of the Romans and Jews had not dwindled. In fact, it continued to grow.

When Paul arrived in Rome, his spiritual children filled him in on the events that had taken place. They told him about the horrific persecution and execution of Christian residents (surely, Paul recalled how he had persecuted Christians while he himself was living in the «dark»). The news sunk him into deep thought...). If he had wanted to spare his life, he would have left the city. There was no way that Paul would run to save his life. «*For to me, to live is Christ, and to die is gain*» (Phil. 1:21), wrote Paul.

Paul rented a small home on the island of Tiber (where a church in his name stands to this day). He found an empty wheat barn which he used to preach to the people. His remaining spiritual children would run to the barn, which was a place of spiritual satisfaction. Many soldiers took a liking to him and they also went to the barn to hear him preach.

One day, the authorities arrived and arrested Paul while he was preaching. He was told that he was being arrested for being the leader of the Christian mob that set the city on fire. Paul was put in shackles and into prison until being questioned (2 Tim. 2:9).

Paul was placed in a dark basement dungeon that was full of human faeces and filth. Even the emperors admitted that their prisons were sheer torture. Many prisoners could not withstand the conditions and died. Paul managed to survive. His faith in the Lord gave him strength.

The cold, damp conditions burdened his frail body. He asked for his cloak which he left in Troas (2 Tim. 4:12). He also asked to see Timothy (2 Tim. 4:12) and Mark (2 Tim. 4:11).

The Apostle had been abandoned by everyone. Luke was the only one to visit him in prison. The Christians of the city «disappeared» as a result of Nero's relentless persecution.

They were not able to find the strength to withstand the emperor's actions and so they went into «hiding». Paul defended himself alone at the hearing. There were no witnesses to come to his defense. Being human, he expressed his feelings to his beloved disciple, Timothy who had stood by him like a son (Phil. 2:22). He wrote: «*At my first defense no one stood with me, but all forsook me. May it not be charged against them. But the Lord stood with me and strengthened me… Also I was delivered out of the mouth of the lion*» (2 Tim. 4:16-17).

Paul was thrown into prison again until being questioned a second time. This time, however, he was paid an unexpected visit. Onesiphorus (who waited for the Apostle Paul and Barnabas at the gate of Iconium 17 years earlier) travelled from Ephesus to Rome in search of Paul. He finally uncovered his whereabouts and he stayed with him and served him. «*The Lord grant mercy to the household of Onesiphorus, for he often refreshed me, and was not ashamed of my chain; but when he arrived in Rome, he sought me out very zealously and found me. The Lord grant to him that he may find mercy from the Lord in that Day…*» (2 Tim. 1:16-18).

19.2. **PAUL ASKS FOR TIMOTHY**

Paul was aware that he was living his last moments on earth. Before he died, he deeply desired to see his beloved son Timothy, who was serving the Church in Ephesus. He wrote a letter to Timothy (the second epistle to Timothy), telling him to come to him as quickly as possible (2 Tim. 4:9). It was his last breath of air. «*To Timothy, a beloved son… I thank God, whom I serve with a pure conscience, as my forefathers did, as without ceasing I remember you in my prayers night and day, greatly desiring to see you, being mindful of your tears, that I may be filled with joy...»* (2 Tim. 1:2-4).

For God has not given us a spirit of fear, but of power and of love and of a sound mind. Therefore do not be ashamed of the testimony of our Lord, nor of me His prisoner, but share with me in the sufferings for the gospel according to the power of God... (2 Tim. 1:7-9). *For... the time of my departure is at hand. I have fought the good fight, I have finished the race, I have kept the faith. Finally, there is laid up for me the crown of righteousness, which the Lord, the righteous Judge, will give to me on that Day, and not to me only but also to all who have loved His appearing* (2 Tim. 4:6-8). *Be diligent to come to me quickly; Get Mark and bring him with you... The Lord Jesus Christ be with your spirit* (2 Tim. 4:9,11,21).

Timothy, however, did not manage to reach Rome in time to see Paul.

19.3. PAUL IS BEHEADED

It was the autumn of 67 AD. Paul's second questioning was over. He had been found guilty of being the leader of the dangerous Christian ideology. He was sentenced to death by decapitation, for he was a Roman citizen. Paul had truly given all he had for Christ.

Most people would consider Paul's death an inglorious one, given how great a man he was. However, Paul considered his death a golden crown. He considered it gain to die for Christ (Phil. 1:21). His death was an imitation of Christ's death. His place of execution was a place of relief and glory. It was not a place of death. It was a place of Life!

Armed guards took Paul out of his prison cell and led him by his shackles to his place of execution, a quiet place which was outside the city. They blindfolded him, made him kneel down and placed his head on a tree stump. Paul's head was then cut off. Paul's head fell to the ground. His body may have been dead but his spirit was alive. In fact, his spirit was much livelier now because it was unified with Christ who is Life!

The events that took place after Paul's execution were unheard of. Only God can perform such actions. When Paul's head was cut off, instead of blood flowing form his neck, everyone was shocked to see milk flowing from his body (which was a sign of purity). There was more to follow. Paul's decapitated head «leaped» forward four times, stopping to face to the north, south, east and west. Four springs of water appeared at the four positions his head jumped to. These springs exist to this very day and are reminiscent of the spiritual water (his life-giving teachings) which Paul «irrigated» the «arid» world with. The Apostle Paul continues to do so to this very day.

Conclusion

Paul's essence was made up of two «persons» who were at odds with each other. Prior to his conversion, he was a persecutor of Christ. After his conversion, he devoted his entire being to Christ and pushed himself to the limit for Christ. After his conversion his life was constantly under threat. Before his conversion he was a threat to other people's lives.

As a persecutor of Christians, no one could dare question his actions. He truly believed he was walking a straight path. Anyone walking a different path was wrong. He based his arguments on Scripture (which he had learned by heart). The first sign of evidence that he was misled was the fact that he would not listen to anyone whose opinion differed. He also possessed an extremely self-confident attitude. He refused to listen to Stephen, even though his face glowed like an angel's! The second sign of evidence that he was misled was his fanaticism. He was so thirsty for blood, his thirst was insatiable.

After his conversion, his self-confidence was replaced by humility. His fanaticism also gave way to love. He did not simply believe in Christ, he became His Apostle. One might assume that Paul may have been misled. Was Paul on the right path? Paul himself provided the answer to this question: *«Even though we have known Christ according to the flesh, yet now we know Him thus no longer»* (2 Cor. 5:16). Paul meant that he no longer saw Christ through his desires, his bias and his experiences. He now looked at Christ objectively. He looked at him as He truly is, the Savior of the world!

If one were to ask Paul if he had a clear conscience when he was persecuting Christians, he would definitely have answered yes because he was fighting on behalf of his faith. As an Apostle, his conscience was also clear. The difference was, as a persecutor, his conscience could be likened to that of a swamp in which the water is still but murky inside. His conscience was like a pool of water that is still and clear, so clear he could see his reflection.

Opening Your Heart to the Gift of God through Major Existential Questions

In this book are collected texts that masterfully comprise both a profound knowledge and the major existential questions of humankind. The texts flow with a simplicity of rare beauty, and the result could not be better: spirituality is presented through a new lens, attracting, instigating and enchanting readers who want to broaden their horizons. As a master of the word, Rubem Alves relates events and experiences in life where God, religiosity, love, beauty and the meaning of life are always present. The author draws transparent and multicolor stained glass windows, using as raw material the existence and the multiple faces of God.

A pedagogue, poet, philosopher, theologian and psychoanalyst, Rubem Alves is one of Brazil's most respected intellectuals. He is a prolific writer —with more than fifty titles in different languages— and one of the most brilliant craftsmen of the Portuguese language.

BUY IT AT:

www.conviviumpress.com

Transparencies of Eternity
RUBEM ALVES
ISBN: 978-1-934996-19-5
136 Pages
Series Sapientia

A Beautiful and Simple Proposal to Construct Our Spiritual Life through Discernment and Prayer of the Heart

One of the greatest experts in the spirituality of Eastern Christianity, Cardinal Špidlík, deals in this book with prayer and spiritual life, with the experience of grace and goodness, through discernment of evil and human passions in everyday experience. It is a beautiful and simple proposal to construct our spiritual life through discernment and prayer of the heart.

Tomáš Špidlík was born in Boskovice, now in the Czech Republic, in 1919. In 1951, Špidlík began broadcasting programs from Vatican Radio calling for freedom behind the Iron Curtain. He met with Alexander Dubcek, former First Secretary of the Central Committee of the Communist Party of Czechoslovakia, and Václav Havel, who became President of Czechoslovakia. Špidlík is Professor of Eastern Spiritual Theology, and Cardinal, and is known as one of the greatest experts in Eastern Christianity today. He has been chosen «Man of the Year, 1990» and «the most admired person of the decade» by the American Bibliographical Institute *of Raleigh in North Carolina.*

BUY IT AT:

www.conviviumpress.com

The Art of Purifying the Heart
Tomáš Špidlík
ISBN: 978-1-934996-18-8
112 Pages
Series Sapientia

Rediscover the Historical Praxis of Jesus through the Latest Research

A provocative and sensitive bestseller

This controversial book is now available in English for the first time. In this bestseller, greeted with both enthusiasm and controversy in Europe, Pagola, criticized by some of depicting a too-human Jesus, offers a scholarly and thought-provoking biblical rereading of the life of Jesus. Pagola reconstructs the complete historical figure of Jesus with a scholarly exegetical and theological approach, in an easy to read language.

José Antonio Pagola was born in Spain in 1937. He completed his theological studies at the Pontifical Gregorian University and his studies in Sacred Scripture at the Pontifical Biblical Institute in Rome. He also studied Biblical sciences at the École Biblique in Jerusalem. He has dedicated his life to Biblical studies and Christology and has done research on the historical Jesus for more than 30 years, selling more than 60,000 copies of his recent theological bestseller *Jesús. Aproximación histórica*, now available in English by Convivium Press.

BUY IT AT:

www.conviviumpress.com

Jesus. An Historical Approximation
JOSÉ A. PAGOLA
ISBN: 978-1-934996-12-6
568 Pages
Series Kyrios

Is Life in Society Possible without Morality?

Sergio Bastianel answers the question by addressing the responsibility of Christians to confront issues of justice within society in ways that promote the common good. The author, who views one's relationship with the «other» as foundational to the moral experience, places a priority on human relationships based on sharing and solidarity. He emphasizes the interconnections between personal morals and social justice and raises fundamental questions about such issues as political life and economics, about hunger and development, and about the true meaning of «charity», all of which are relevant issues in our contemporary societies.

Sergio Bastianel s.j. is currently professor of moral theology at the Pontifical Gregorian University in Rome and also serves as its academic vice-rector. He spent his early years teaching and lecturing at the Pontifical Theological Faculty of San Luigi in Naples, Italy, and in later years he served as dean of the theological faculty of the Pontifical Gregorian University.

BUY IT AT:

www.conviviumpress.com

Morality in Social Life
Sergio Bastianel
ISBN: 978-1-934996-14-0
360 Pages
Series Episteme

Understanding the unique Priesthood of Jesus Christ for the first Christian communities

In this work by Albert Vanhoye, a detailed analysis of the text known as the Epistle to the Hebrews enables us to conclude without a shadow of a doubt that this is the full text of a splendid Christian preaching, which constantly conforms to the rules of Semitic rhetoric, including various genres of parallelism, synonymis, antithesis and complementarity, and obeying a concentrically symmetrical schema.

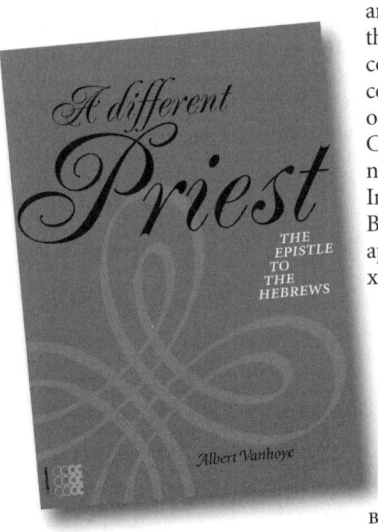

Albert Vanhoye is one of the most recognized scholars on the Epistle to the Hebrews. He has taught it at the Pontifical Biblical Institute and published a great number of specialist articles and books on it, and now brings one of the most contemporary authoritative commentaries to a wider audience, contributing with the understanding of the unique Priesthood of Jesus Christ for the first Christian communities. He is honorary president of the International Society for the study of Biblical and Semitic Rhetoric. He was appointed Cardinal by Pope Benedict XVI in 2006.

BUY IT AT:

www.conviviumpress.com

A Different Priest:
The Epistle to the Hebrews
ALBERT VANHOYE
ISBN: 978-1-934996-20-1
456 Pages
Series Rhetorica Semitica

A new reading of freedom and liberation through Israel's History

Rediscovering freedom in the Bible

Meynet posits that the concept of freedom in the Hebrew Bible is the guiding core of all the socio-political distinctions within Israel's religious experience and history. This original study leads us through the experience of the people of Israel in the Exodus. It guides us into a new reading of the Law in the two narrative sections of the Decalogue, seeing it as an expression of the search for the authentic meaning of human freedom. He also introduces Israel's Psalms as hymns of freedom.

Roland Meynet S.J. is presently professor of Biblical theology at the Pontifical Gregorian University in Rome and was the former director of its Department of Biblical Theology. He is a founding member and currently the secretary of the International Society for the Studies of Biblical and Semitic Rhetoric.

BUY IT AT:

www.conviviumpress.com

Called to freedom
ROLAND MEYNET
ISBN: 978-1-934996-08-9
296 Pages
Series Rhetorica Semitica

A new perspective to study the Gospels of Mark, Matthew and Luke

Meynet offers an entirely new perspective on the study of the Synoptic Gospels, adding further insights within the growing body of modern research into the meanings of the Gospels of Maththew, Mark and Luke. Utilizing the rhetorical method of analysis, of wich he is leading proponent, Meynet studies the composition of the Gospels and makes it possible to understand them in systematic and until now unexpected ways.

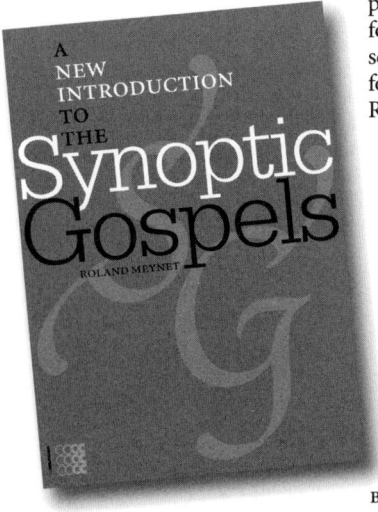

Roland Meynet S.J. is presently professor of Biblical theology at the Pontifical Gregorian University in Rome and was the former director of its Department of Biblical Theology. He is a founding member and currently the secretary of the International Society for the Studies of Biblical and Semitic Rhetoric.

BUY IT AT:

www.conviviumpress.com

A New Introduction to the Synoptic Gospels
Roland Meynet
ISBN: 978-1-934996-11-9
440 Pages
Series Rhetorica Semitica

Reclaiming the spirit and praxis of the reign of God

Post-resurrection communities continued to practice living in the reign of God. With the rise of Emperor Constantine, however, this vibrant counter-cultural movement of believers was institutionalized within the Roman Empire. Over time the institutional Church became the dominant power with all the trappings of empire. The author shows how this notion can change the face of Christianity.

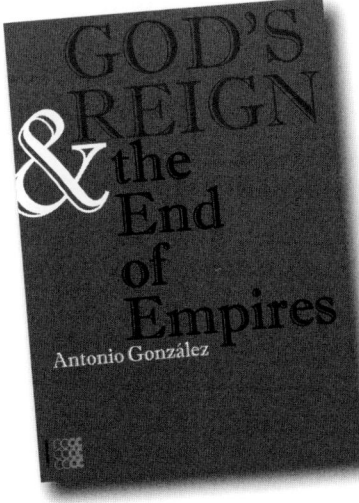

Antonio González, a leading Spanish theologian, was born in Oviedo (Asturias) in 1961. He has worked in El Salvador and in Guatemala at the Jesuit University, as well as in various centers of higher education in Europe. He shares with liberation theology the perspective of God's option for the poor and the centrality of praxis in the Christian message and life. He is a member of the Mennonite community and was the former General Secretary of the Fundacion Xavier Zubiri in Madrid, Spain. González is a prolific author whose works include *Structures in Praxis* (1997), *Trinity and Liberation* (1993), and more recently, *Theology of the Evangelical Praxis*.

BUY IT AT:

www.conviviumpress.com

God's Reign & the End of Empires
ANTONIO GONZÁLEZ
ISBN: 978-1-934996-29-4
Series Kyrios

Paul: The Great Scandal

This book was printed on *thin opaque smooth white Bible paper*, using the *Minion* and *Type Embellishments One* font families.

This edition was printed in D'VINNI, S.A., in Bogotá, Colombia, during the last weeks of the sixth month of year two thousand twelve.

Ad publicam lucem datus mense junii Sacri Cordis Iesus